AA

GLOVEBOX ATLAS
BRITAIN

Reprinted April 1998
Reprinted February 1998
Reprinted November 1997
Reprinted August 1997
2nd reprint July 1997
Reprinted July 1997
Reprinted June 1997
Reprinted May 1997
Reprinted April 1997
Reprinted February 1997
Reprinted January 1997
Reprinted October 1996
Reprinted August 1996
2nd reprint June 1996
Reprinted June 1996
4th edition June 1996
3rd edition April 1994
Reprinted June 1994
Reprinted August 1994
Reprinted September 1994
Reprinted November 1994
Reprinted January 1995
Reprinted February 1995
Reprinted March 1995
Reprinted May 1995
Reprinted with amendments July 1995
Reprinted September 1995
Reprinted October 1995
Reprinted January 1996
2nd edition October 1992
Reprinted January 1993
Reprinted March 1993
Reprinted August 1993
Reprinted December 1993
1st edition May 1990
Reprinted with amendments April 1991

© The Automobile Association 1996

Published by AA Publishing (a trading name of
Automobile Association Developments Limited,
whose registered office is Norfolk House, Priestley
Road, Basingstoke, Hampshire RG24 9NY. Registered
number 1878835).

Mapping produced by the Cartographic Department
of The Automobile Association. This atlas has been
compiled and produced from the Automaps database
utilising electronic and computer technology.

ISBN 0 7495 1309 8, 0 7495 1308 X

A CIP Catalogue record for this book is available
from the British Library.

Printed by BPC Waterlow Ltd, Dunstable.

The contents of this atlas are believed correct at the
time of printing. Nevertheless, the publishers cannot
be held responsible for any errors or omissions, or
for changes in the details given. They would welcome
information to help keep this atlas up to date; please
write to the Cartographic Editor, Publishing Division,
The Automobile Association, Priestley Road,
Basingstoke, Hampshire RG24 9NY.

contents

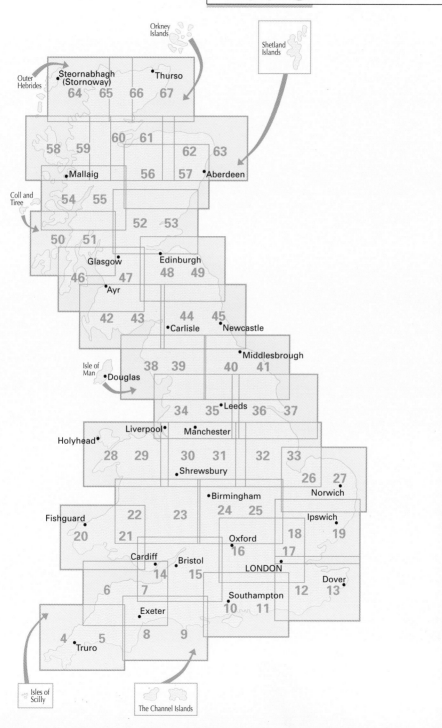

map symbols

Britain

▭M3▭	Motorway with number	☼M3☼ 5 6 7	Distance in miles between symbols
⊕	Motorway junction with and without number	– ▼ –	Vehicle ferry – Great Britain
●	Motorway junction with limited access	▼ BERGEN	Vehicle ferry – Continental
⬤S Fleet	Motorway service area	⊞ CALAIS	Hovercraft ferry
▭▭▭	Motorway under construction	▬▬▬▬	National boundary
▭A31▭	Primary route single/dual carriageway	Ⓗ	Heliport
▭S▭	Primary route service area	✈	Airport
A33	Other A road single/dual carriageway	☎	AA telephone
B4224	B road single/dual carriageway	☎	BT telephone in isolated places
▭▭▭	Unclassified road	AA	AA Shops
■■□■■	Road under construction	☀	Viewpoint
▬▬▬ ▬▬▬ = = = =	Narrow primary, other A or B road with passing places (Scotland)	▲ SNAEFELL 620	Spot height in metres
TOLL	Road toll	23	Page overlap with number

scale

1: 500 000

8 miles : 1 inch

0   5   10 miles
0   5   10   15 kilometres

Ireland

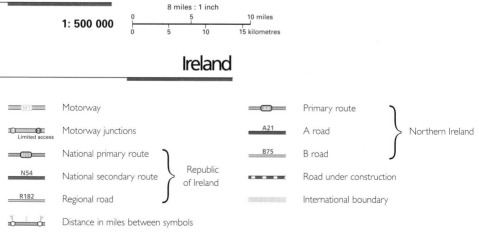

▭M1▭	Motorway
⊞ ⊞ Limited access	Motorway junctions
▭N▭	National primary route
N54	National secondary route
R182	Regional road
⊞ S ⊞	Distance in miles between symbols

Republic of Ireland

▭A▭	Primary route
A21	A road
B75	B road
■■■■	Road under construction
▬▬▬▬	International boundary

Northern Ireland

scale

1:1 000 000

16 miles : 1 inch

0   10   20 miles
0   10   20   30 kilometres

using the index

Britain

see pages 79 - 94

Each entry in the index is followed by the atlas page number and then two letters denoting the 100km national grid square. The last two figures refer to the west–east and south–north numbered grid lines.

For example:

Whitchurch **30** SJ54

The letters 'SJ' refer to the major National Grid square. The number '5' refers to the square along the bottom of the page. The number '4' is found up the left–hand side of the page. Whitchurch can be found within the intersecting square.

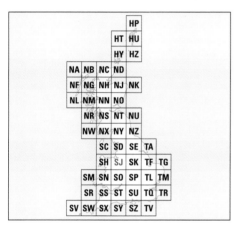

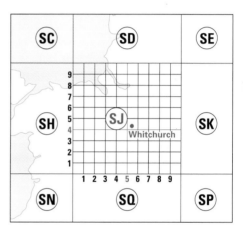

Ireland

see pages 76 - 78

Each placename reference in the index gives the page number first, followed by the letter and number of the square in which the particular place can be found.

For example:

Belfast **71** E3 is located on page 71

The letter 'E' refers to the square along the bottom of the page. The number '3' refers to the square on the left-hand side. Belfast can be found within the intersecting square.

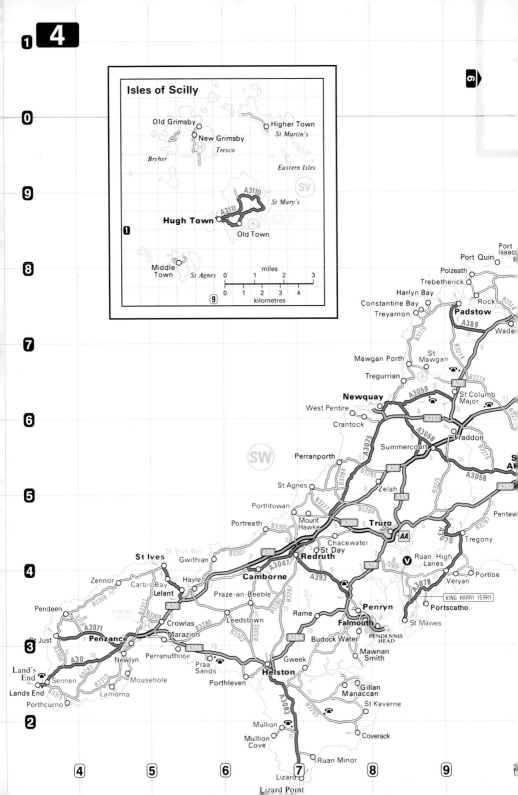

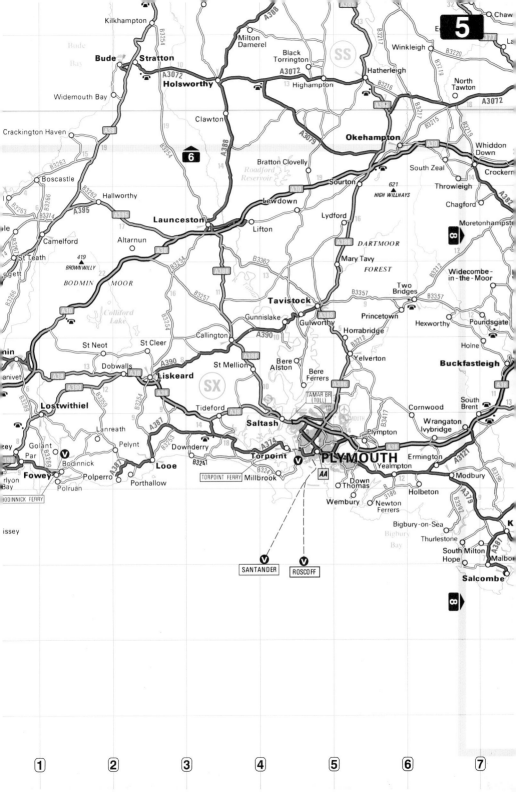

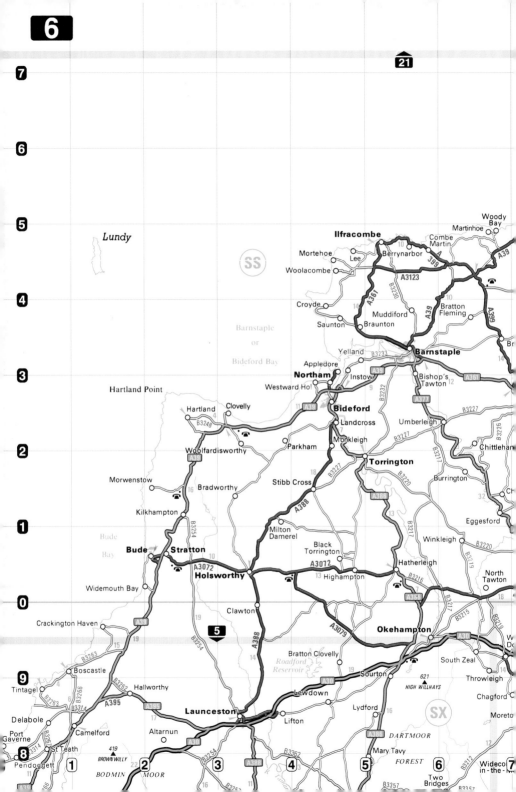

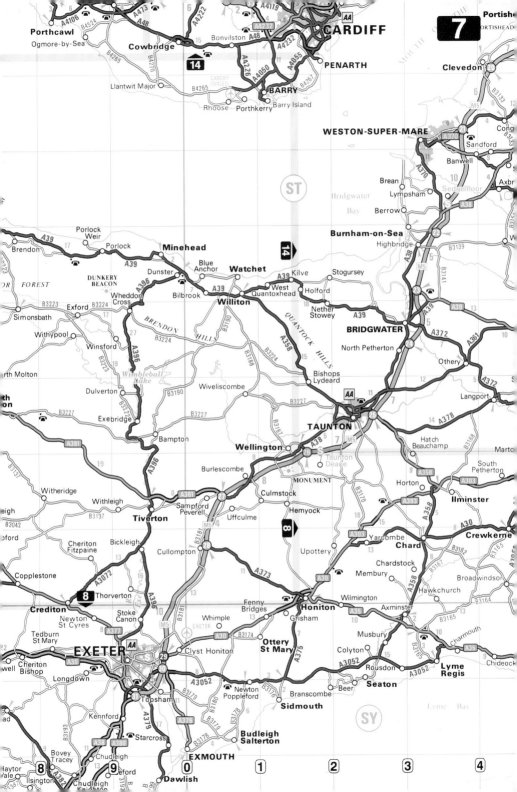

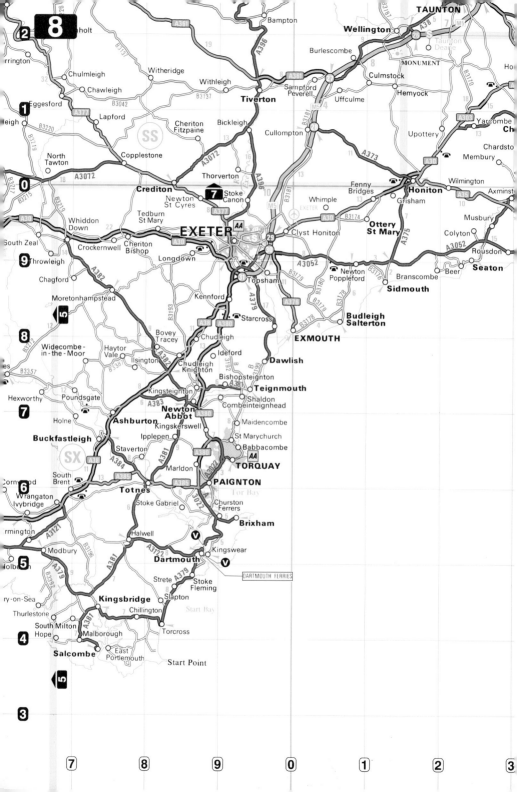

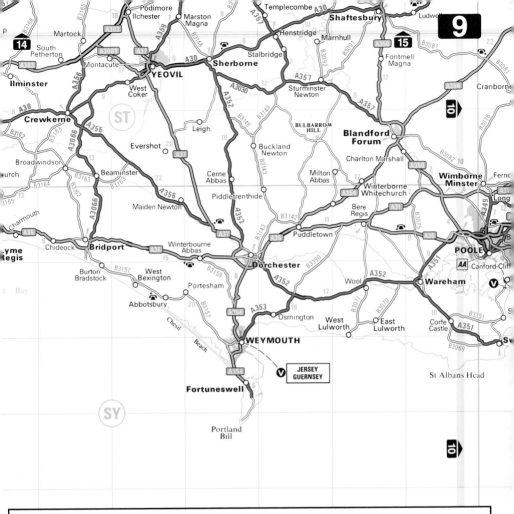

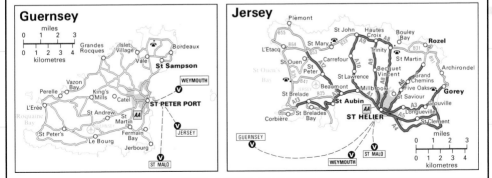

Guernsey

miles
0 1 2 3
0 1 2 3 4
kilometres

Grandes
Rocques
Islet
Village
Bordeaux
Vazon
Bay
Vale
ST Sampson
WEYMOUTH
Perelle
King's
Mills
Catel
ST PETER PORT
L'Erée
St Andrew
AA
Roquaine
Bay
St
Martin
JERSEY
St Peter's
Fermain
Bay
Le Bourg
Jerbourg
ST MALO

Jersey

Piémont
St John
Hautes
Croix
Bouley
Bay
Rozel
L'Etacq
B64
St Mary
St Martin
Archirondel
St Ouen
Carrefour
Trinity
Grand
Chemins
Gorey
St Ouen's
Bay
St Peter
St Lawrence
Becquet
Vincent
Five Oaks
Beaumont
Millbrook
St Saviour
Grouville
St Brelade
St Aubin
Longueville
Corbière
St Brelades
Bay
ST HELIER
St Clement
GUERNSEY
miles
0 1 2 3
0 1 2 3 4
kilometres
WEYMOUTH
ST MALO

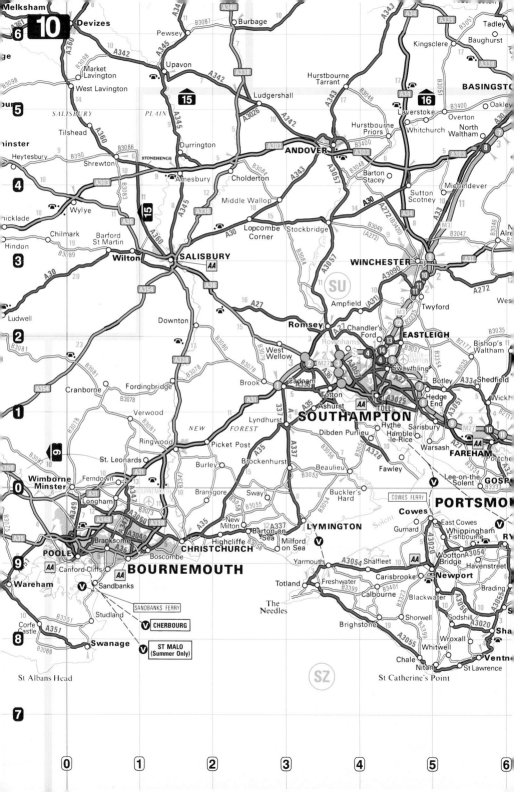

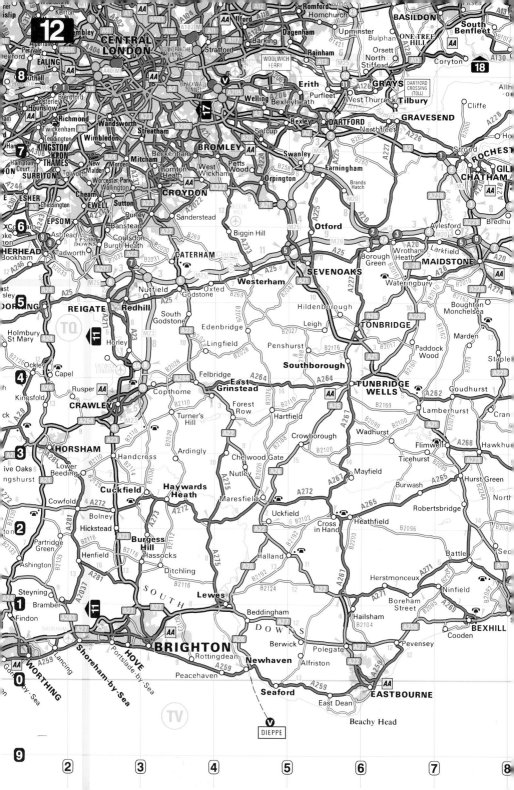

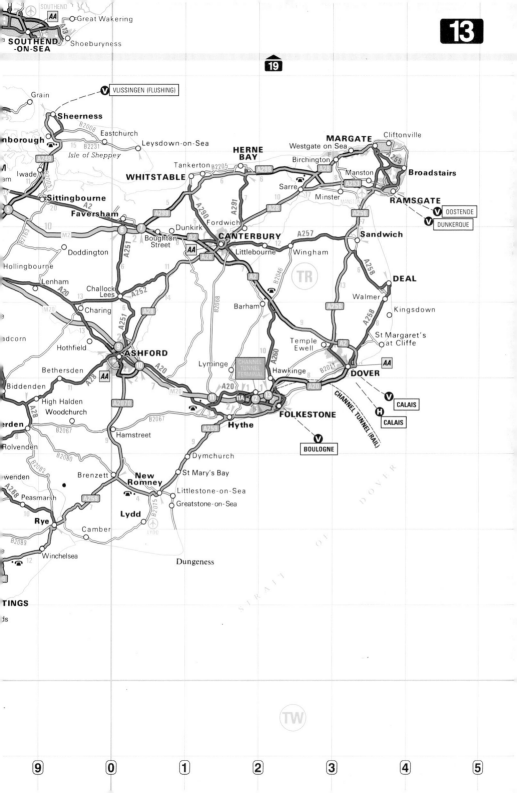

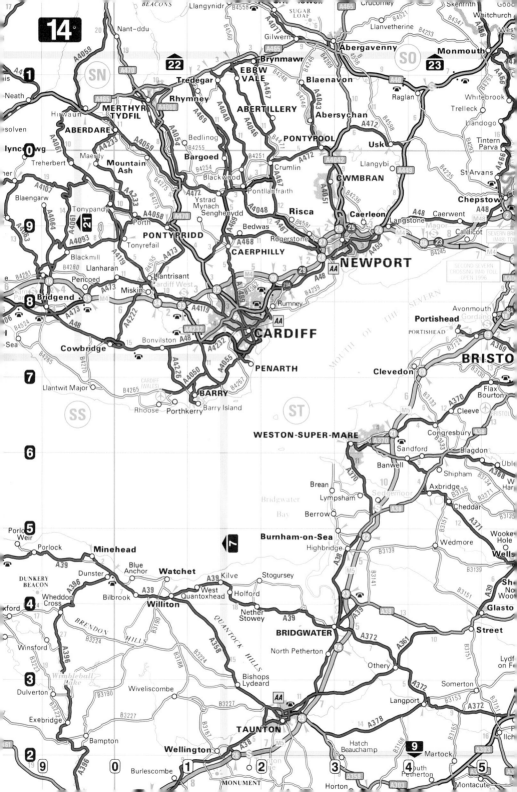

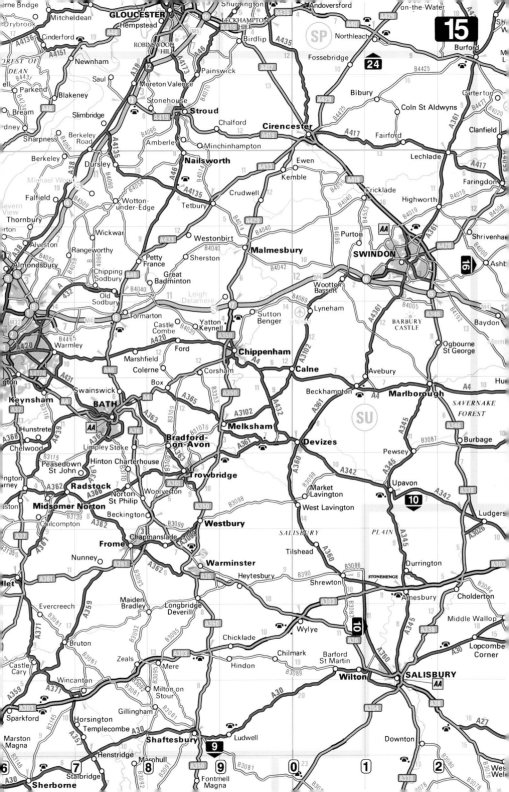

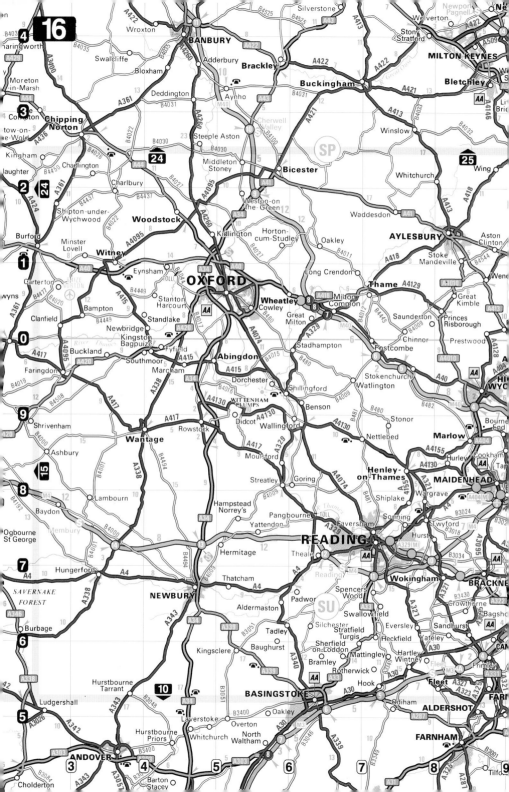

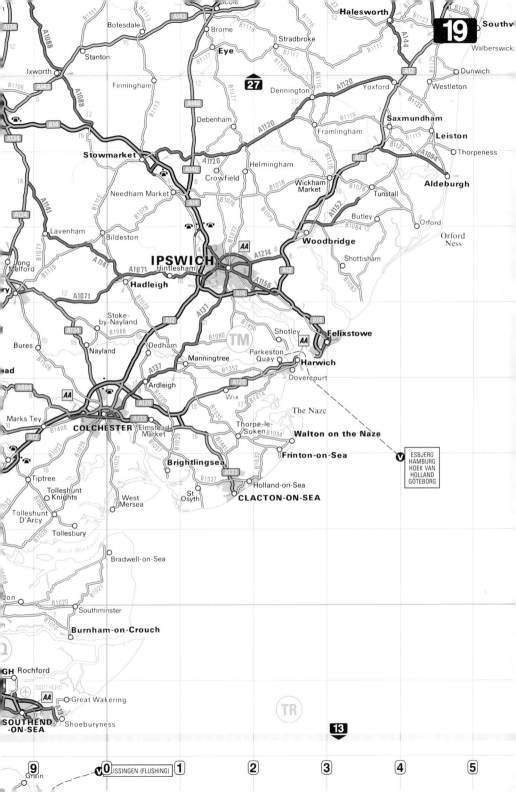

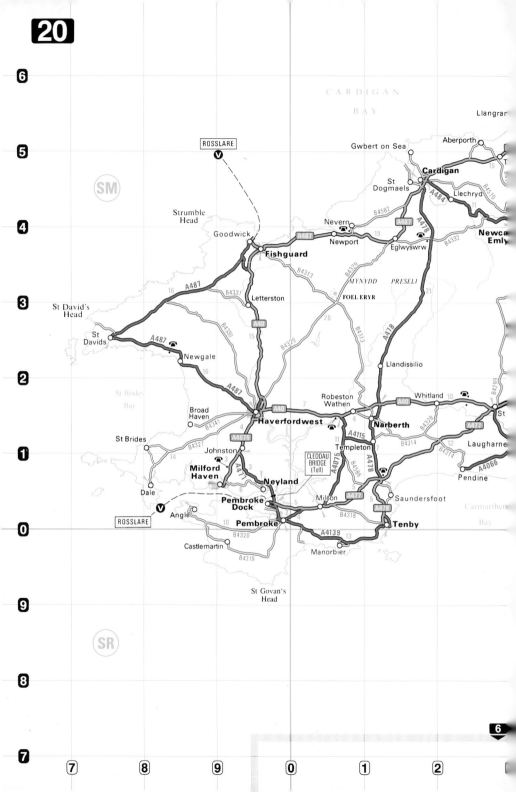

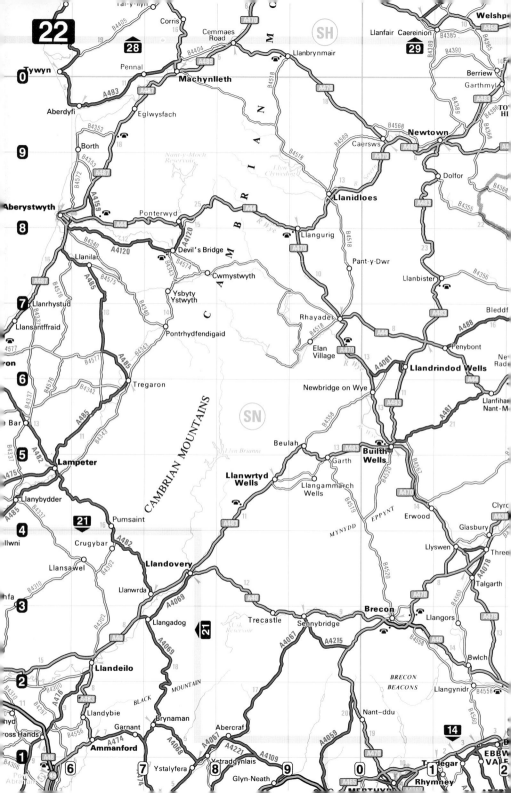

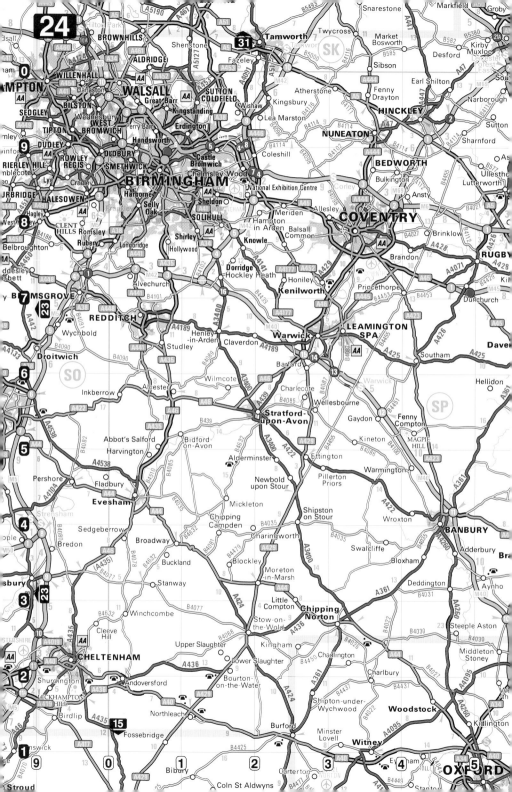

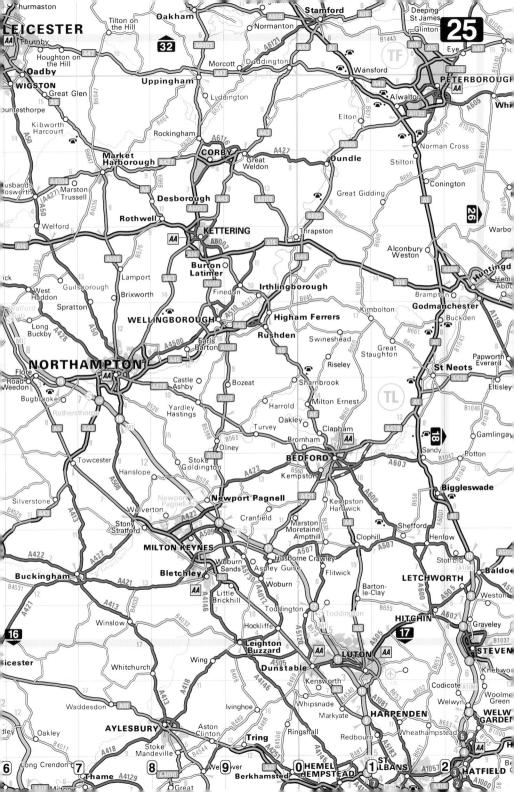

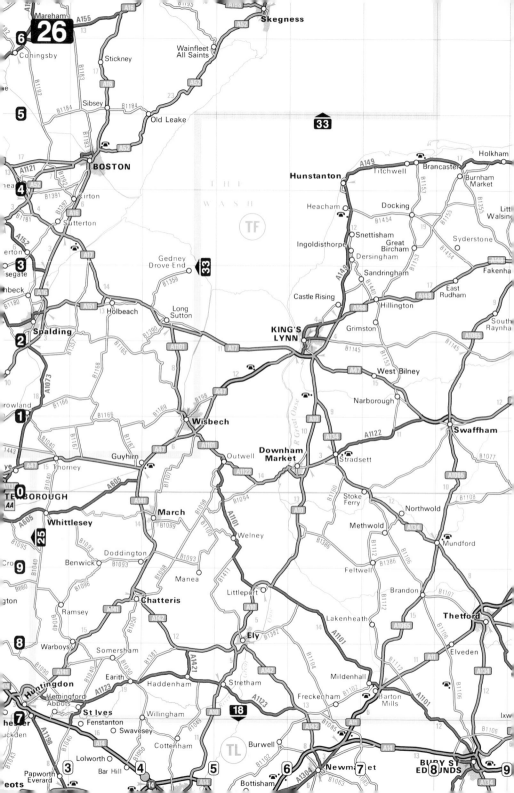

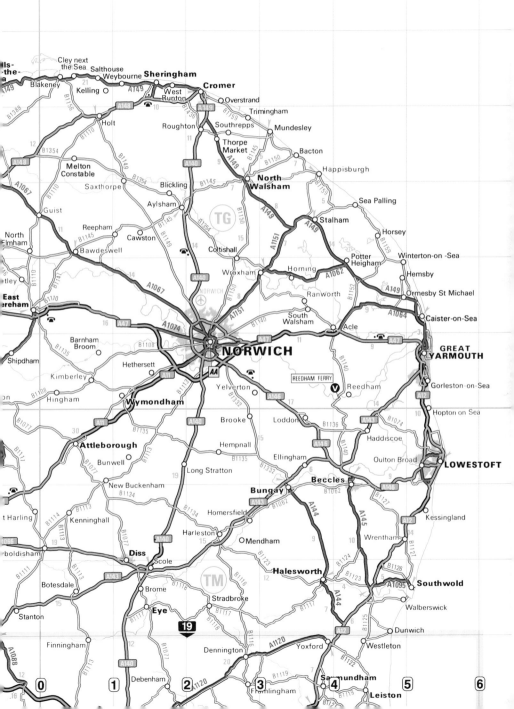

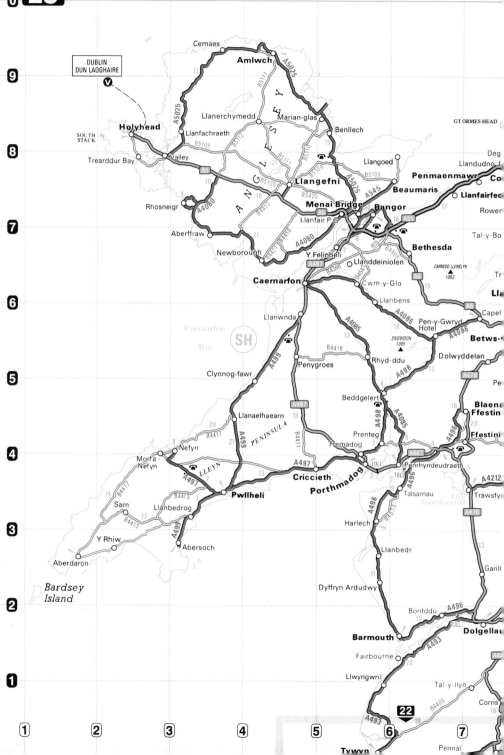

ROTTERDAM (EUROPOORT)
ZEEBRUGGE

Caistor
Waltham
North Cotes
North Somercotes
B1201
A1031
Ludborough
Binbrook
Market Rasen
A631
A631
A157
Saltfleet
A1031
A1200
Louth
37
A157
Mablethorpe
A157
A52
Sutton on Sea
Withern
A1104
A1111
Wragby
A158
A153
Tetford
Alford
A1104
B1449
Chapel St Leonards
Baumber
Ulceby
B1196
A52
Bardney
B1190
Horncastle
A158
Spilsby
Candlesby
Ingoldmells
Woodhall Spa
B1183
Mareham le Fen
A155
A16
B1195
A158
Skegness
Metheringham
A16
Stickney
Wainfleet All Saints
A52
Billinghay
Coningsby
A153
North Kyme
Sibsey
B1184
Old Leake
A52
Heckington
A17
A1121
BOSTON
Hunstanton
A149
Titchwel
Helpringham
Swineshead
A52
Kirton
Heacham
Dockir
B1454
Donington
A152
Sutterton
A16
Ingoldisthorpe
Snettisham
Great Bircha
Dersingham
Gosberton
A17
Gedney Drove End
26
Sandringha
Risegate
B1359
Castle Rising
Hilling
Pinchbeck
A16
Holbeach
Long Sutton
KING'S LYNN
Grimston
Spalding
A17
A47
West B
Bourne
A151
A151
Deeping St Nicholas
A1073
A101
Wisbech
Narborough
Baston
Langtoft
A16
Crowland
Downham Market
A1122
Market Deeping
Deeping St James
26
Guyhirn
Outwell
Stradsett
Glinton
Eye
Thorney
A47
4
5
6
7

THE WASH

TF

26

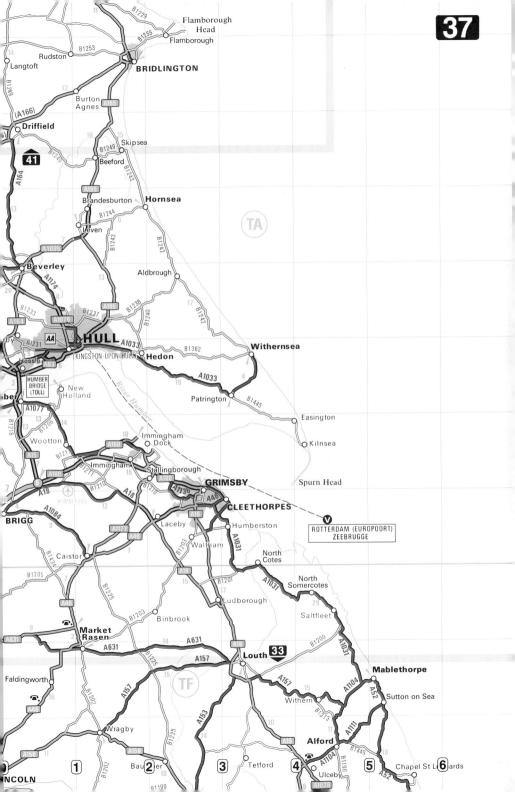

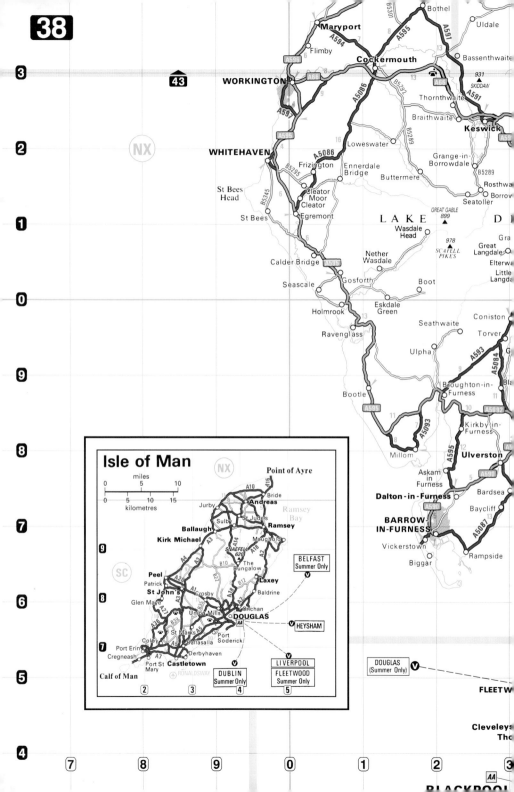

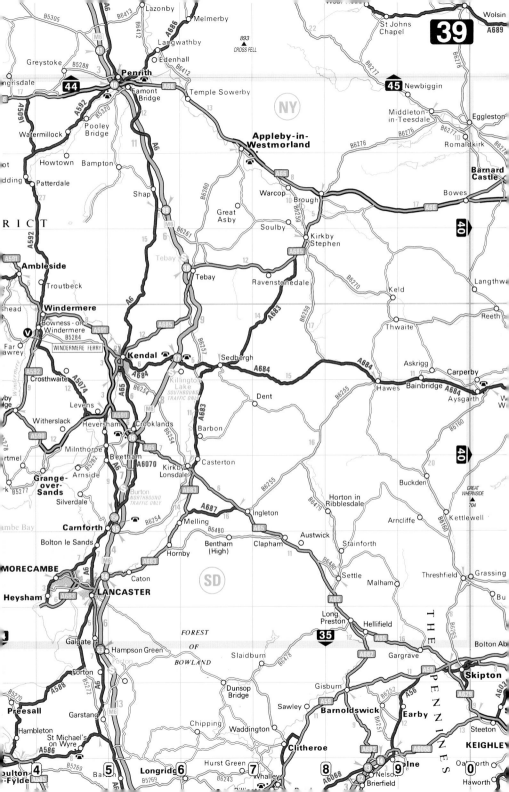

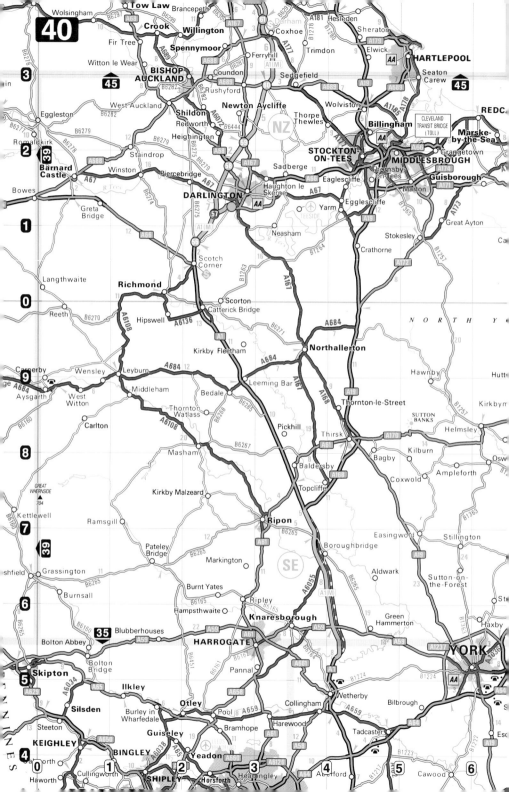

n by the Sea

otton

Easingston Staithes

tus

B1366 B1266 A174 Sandsend

A171 **Whitby**

Ruswarp

Egton Robin Hood's
Bay

Grosmont

Goathland Ravenscar

M O O R S

Rosedale Abbey A171

Cloughton

Lastingham Hackness **Scalby**

Appleton-Le-Moors **SCARBOROUGH**

Wrelton A170

A170 East Ayton Eastfield

Pickering Wykeham B1261

Thornton Seamer

A169 Dale A64 A1039 **Filey**

Kirby B1258 Staxton A165

Misperton Sherburn Hunmanby

ngham B1257 B1249 Reighton

B1229

Malton Rillington Flamborough
Head

B1256 Flamborough

B1248

North Sledmere Rudston B1253 **BRIDLINGTON**

Grimston B1253 Langtoft

B1248 B1249 TA

Fridaythorpe A166 Burton A165

A166 Agnes

(A163) **Driffield**

A614 37

Stamford B1248 A614 B1249 Skipsea

Bridge B1246 Bainton Beeford

A1079 A164

Barmby Pocklington Middleton on Brandesburton **Hornsea**

Moor (A163) the Wolds A165

on A614 B1244

Market Leven

Shiptonthorpe Weighton

A1079 A1035

Holme upon B1278 **Beverley**

Spalding Moor

7 **8** **9** **0** Walkington **1** rough **2** **3**

A163 A1034 A1174

B1230

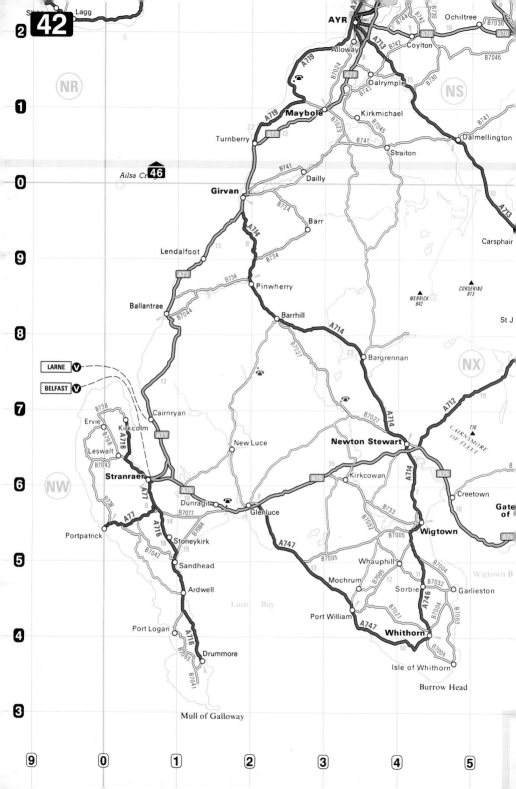

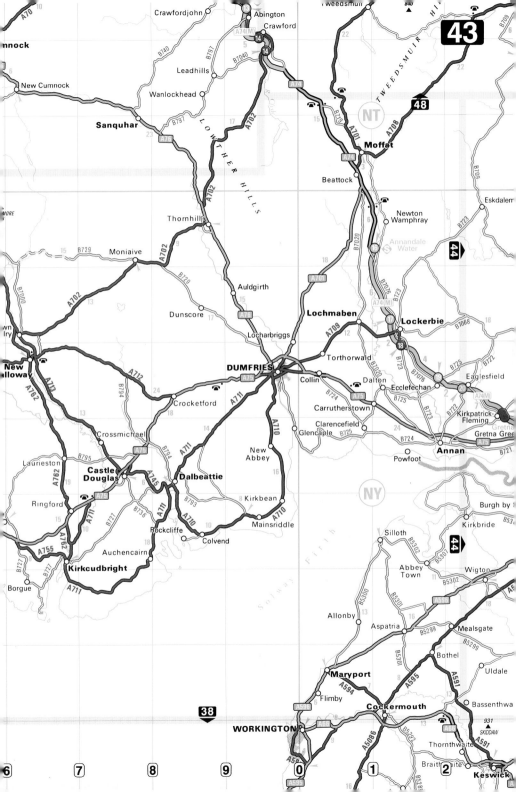

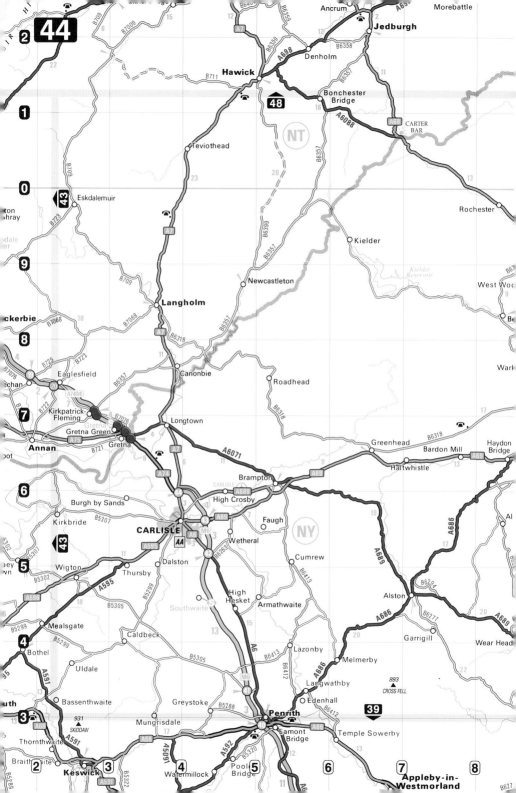

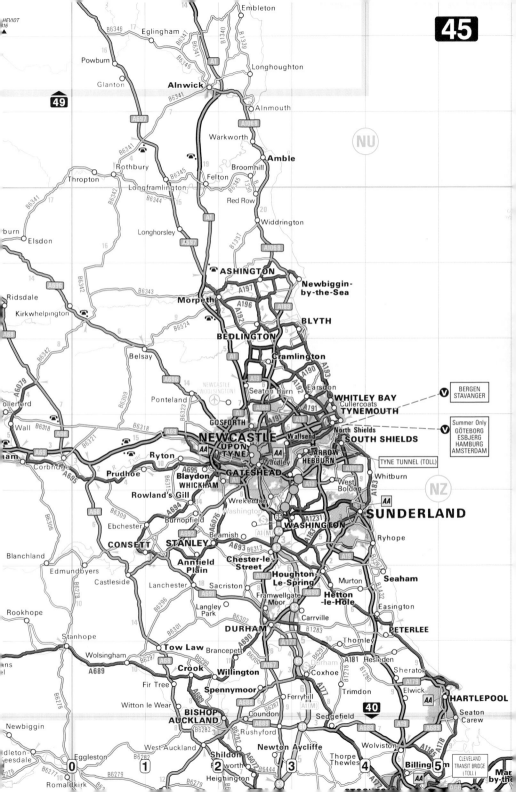

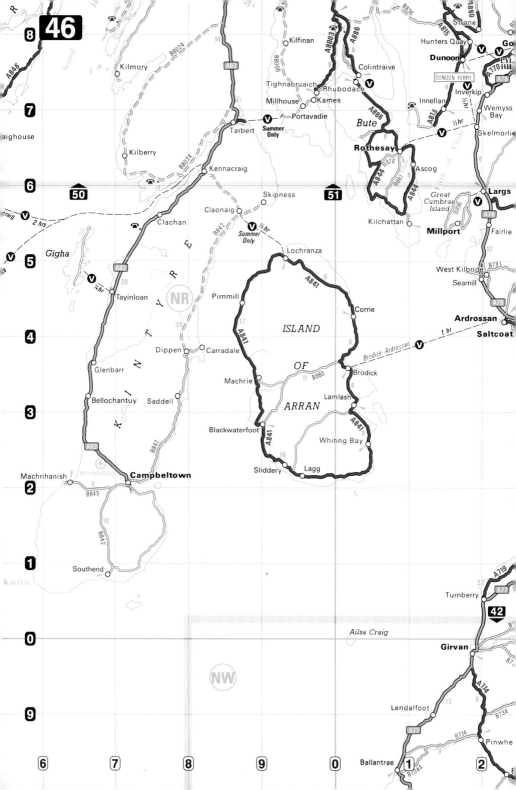

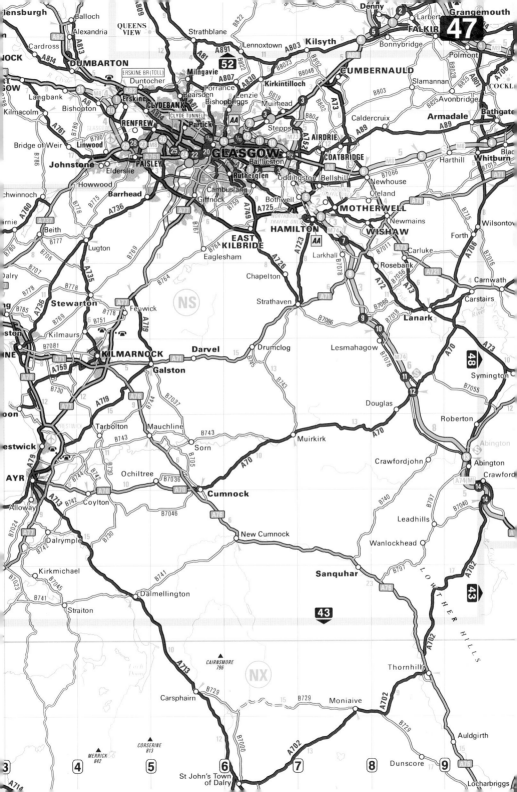

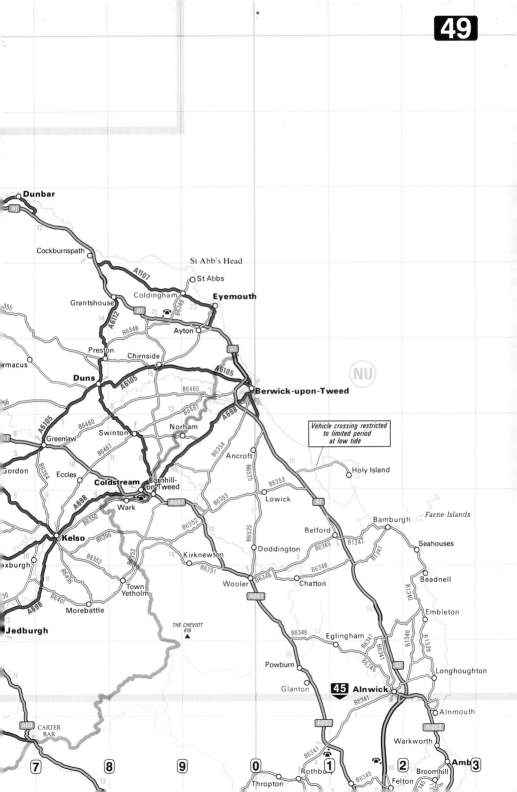

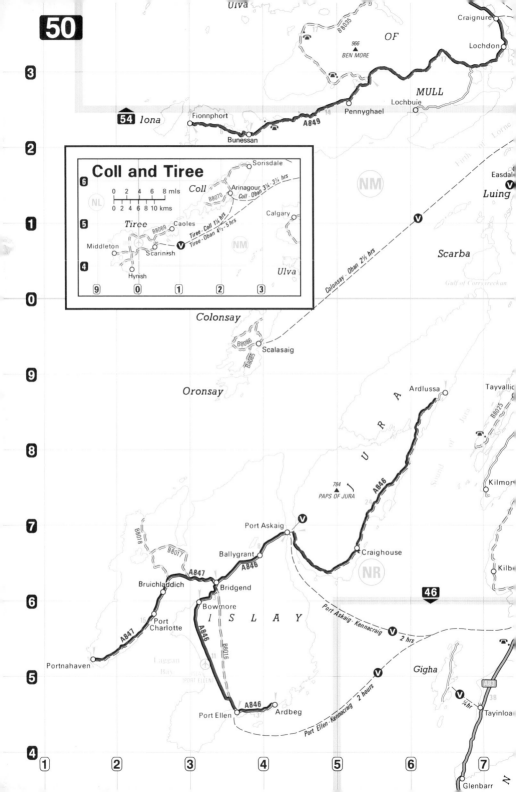

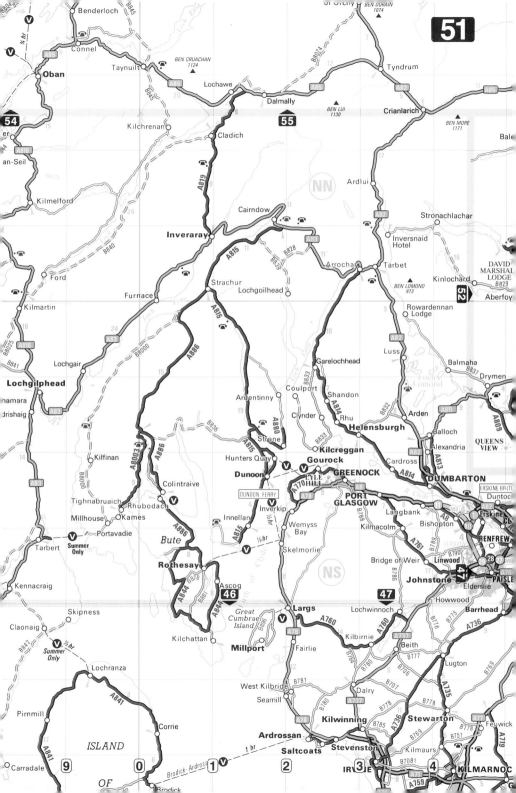

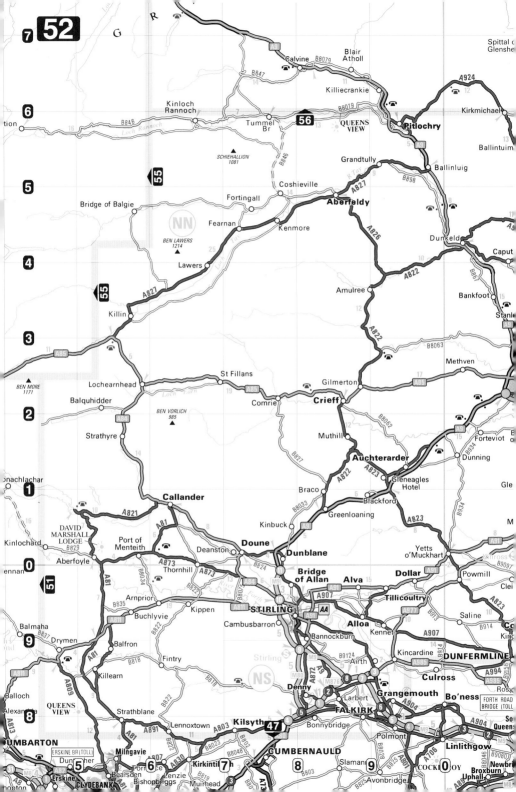

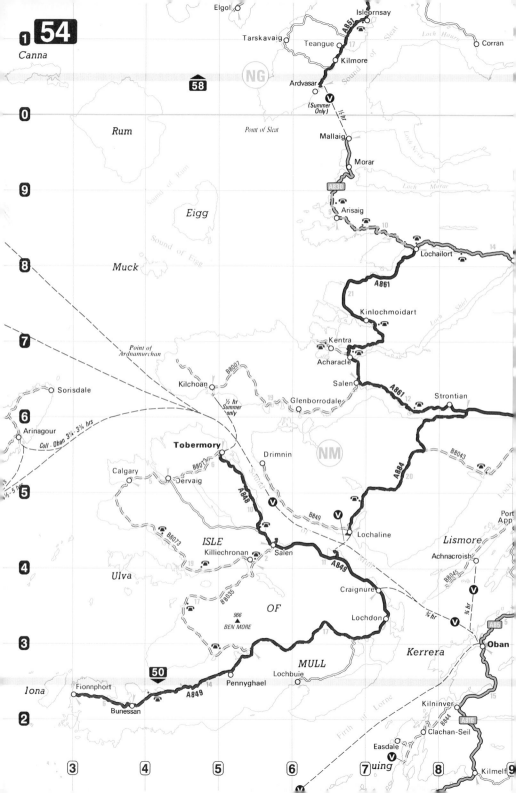

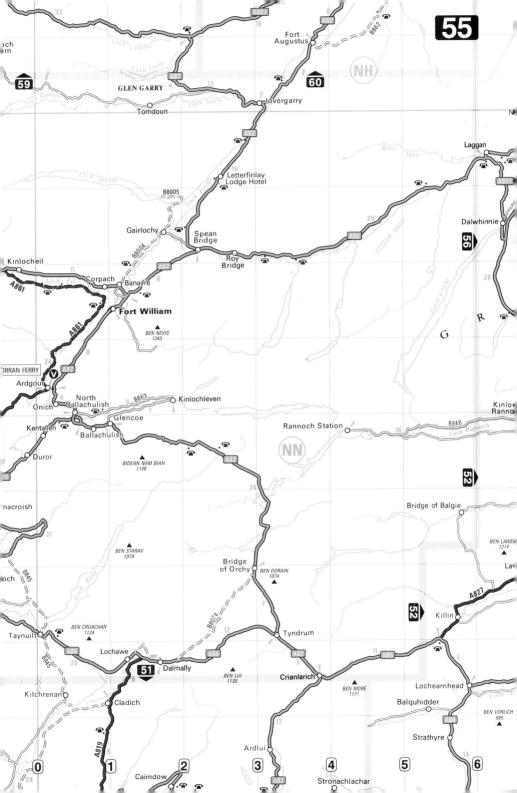

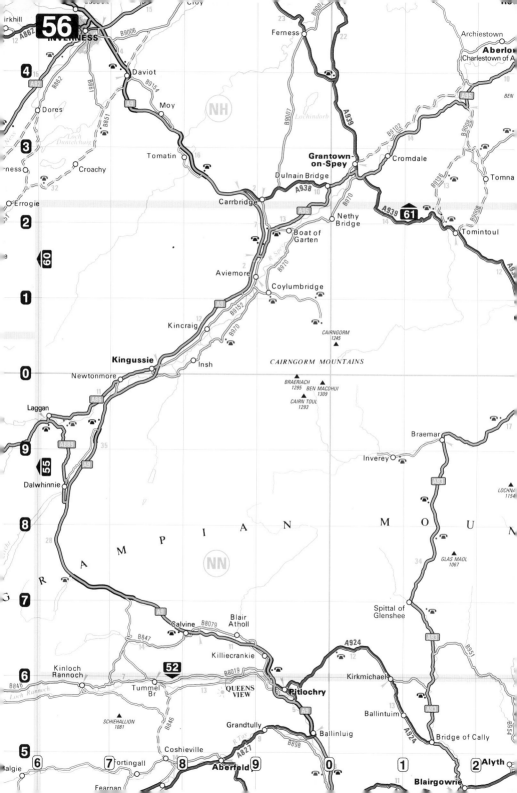

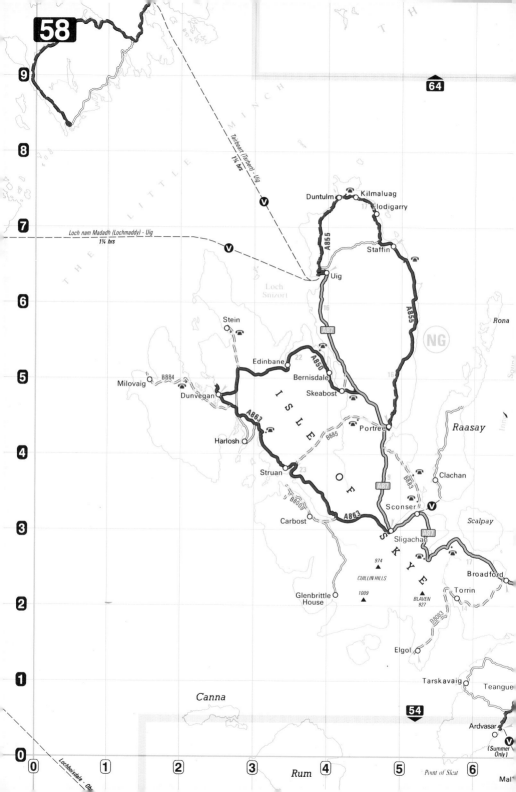

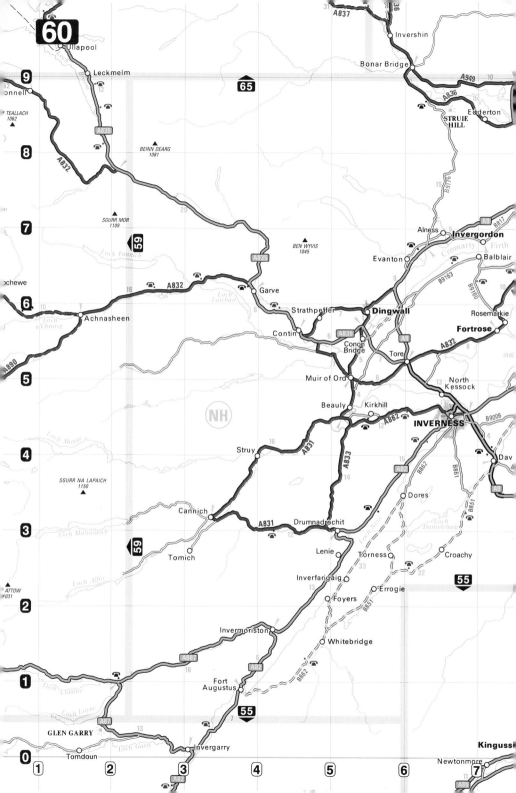

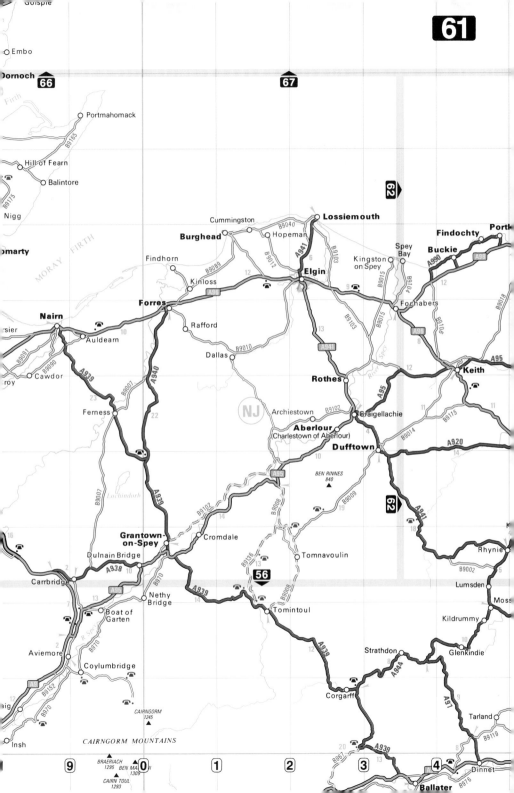

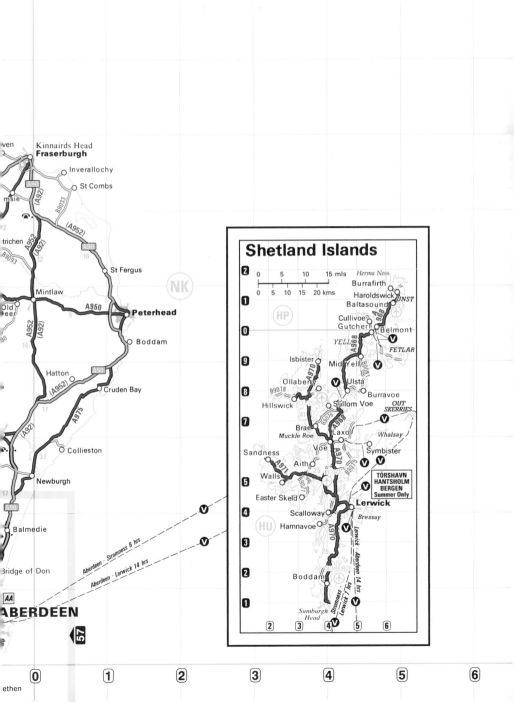

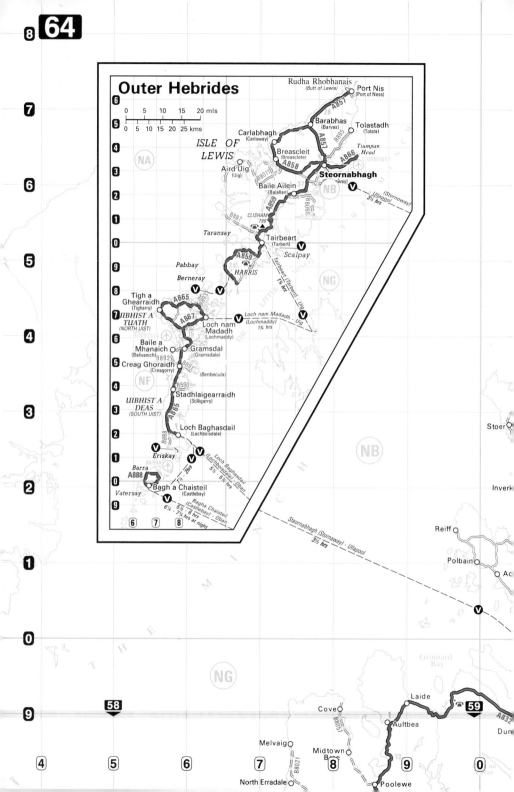

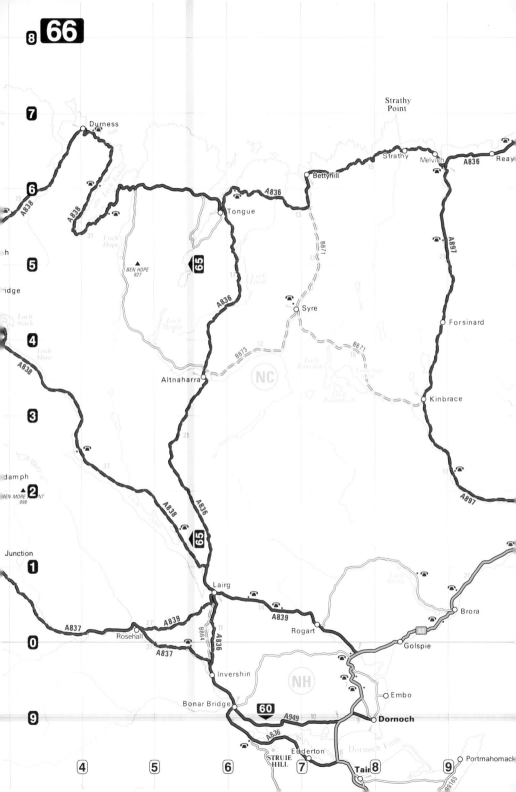

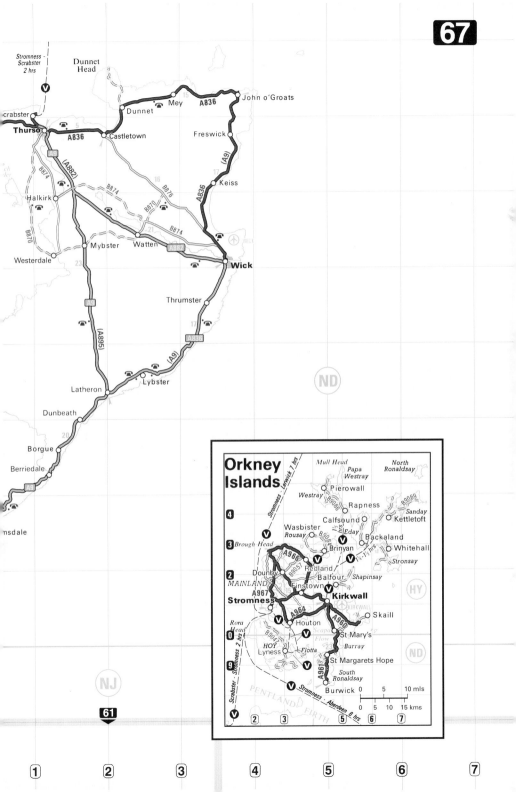

Stromness - Scrabster 2 hrs

Dunnet Head

John o'Groats

V

crabster

Mey A836

Dunnet

Freswick

Thurso

A836

Castletown

(A9)

A836

A9

(A882)

Keiss

B874

Halkirk

B874

B876

B870

B874

Westerdale

Mybster

Watten

A9

Wick

A9

Thrumster

A895

A836

Latheron

(A9)

Lybster

Dunbeath

Borgue

Berriedale

A9

nsdale

ND

NJ

Orkney Islands

Stromness - Lerwick 7 hrs

Mull Head

Papa Westray

North Ronaldsay

4

Pierowall

Westray

Rapness

B9066

3 Brough Head

Wasbister

Rousay

Calfsound

B9057

Eday

V

Sanday

Kettletoft

Backaland

A966

Brinyan

V

Whitehall

2

Dounby

Redland

B9057

Balfour

Shapinsay

Stronsay

MAINLAND

Finstown

Kirkwall

Stromness

A967

A965

KIRKWALL

Skaill

Rora Head

0

Houton

A960

St Mary's

B9047

V

Scapa Flow

Burray

HOY

Lyness

Flotta

St Margarets Hope

9

A961

South Ronaldsay

Scrabster - Stromness 2 hrs

Stromness - Aberdeen 8 hrs

Burwick

0   5   10 mls

0   5   10   15 kms

V

PENTLAND FIRTH

2   3   5   6   7

HY

ND

1   2   3   4   5   6   7

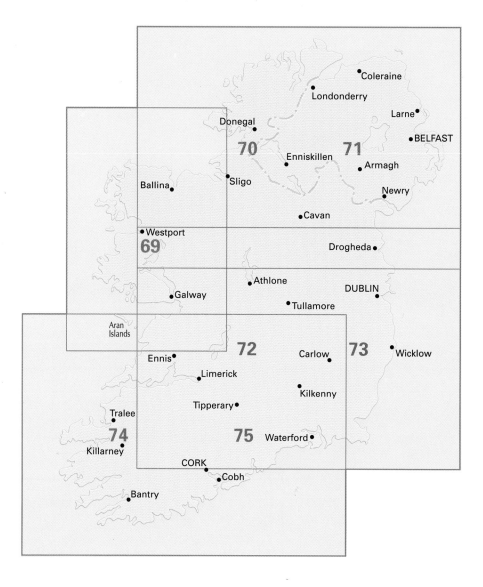

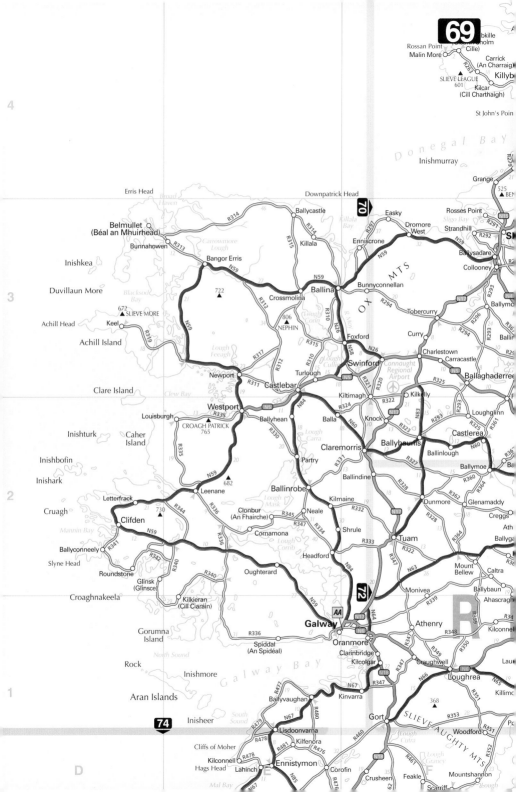

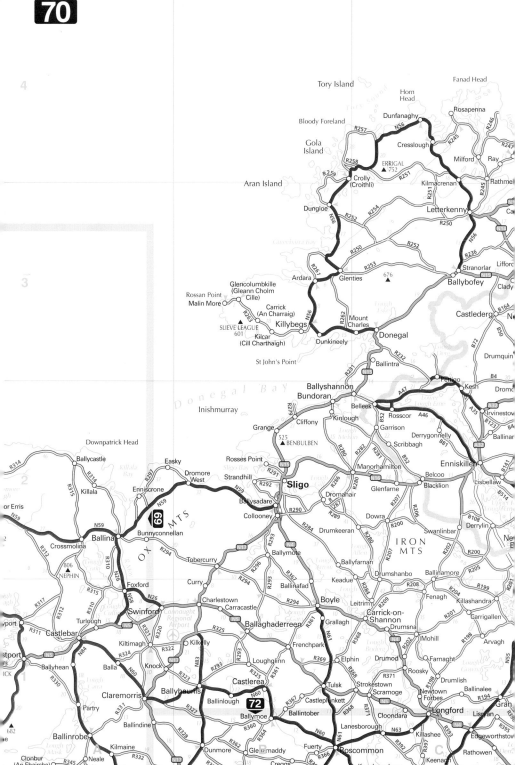

To Douglas (Summer Only)

To Holyhead

To Pembroke Dock

To Fishguard

CHERBOURG
LE HAVRE

Abbeydorney 74 B3
Abbeyfeale 74 C3
Abbeyleix 72 C2
Adamstown 73 D1
Adare 75 D3
Adrigole 74 B2
Ahascragh 72 B3
Ahoghill 71 E3
Allihies 74 B1
Anascaul 74 B2
Annalong 71 E2
Annestown 72 C1
Antrim 71 E3
Ardagh 74 C3
Ardara 70 B3
Ardcath 73 E4
Ardee 71 E1
Ardfert 74 B3
Ardfinnan 72 C1
Ardglass 71 F2
Ardgroom 74 B2
Arklow 73 E2
Arless 73 D2
Armagh 71 D2
Armoy 71 E4
Arthurstown 73 D1
Arvagh 70 C1
Ashbourne 73 E4
Ashford 73 E3
Askeaton 74 C3
Athboy 73 D4
Athea 74 C3
Athenry 72 B3
Athleague 72 B4
Athlone 72 C4
Athy 73 D3
Augher 71 D2
Aughnacloy 71 D2
Aughrim 73 E2
Avoca 73 E2

Bagenalstown
(Muine Bheag) 73 D2
Bailieborough 71 D1
Balbriggan 73 E4
Balla 69 E2
Ballacolla 72 C2
Ballaghaderreen 70 B1
Ballina 69 E3
Ballina 75 D4
Ballinafad 70 B1
Ballinagh 70 C1
Ballinakill 72 C2
Ballinalee 70 C1
Ballinamallard 70 C2
Ballinamore 70 C2
Ballinamore 70 B4
Ballinascarty 74 C1
Ballinasloe 72 B3
Ballindine 72 A4
Ballineen 74 C2
Ballingarry 74 C3
Ballingarry 72 C2
Ballingeary (Béal Atha
an Ghaorthaidh) 74 C2
Ballinhassig 75 D2
Ballinlough 70 B1
Ballinrobe 69 E2
Ballinspittle 75 D1
Ballintober 70 B1
Ballintra 70 C3
Ballivor 73 D4
Ballon 73 D2
Ballybaun 72 B4
Ballybay 71 D2
Ballybofey 70 C3
Ballybunion 74 B3
Ballycanew 73 E2

Ballycarry 71 F3
Ballycastle 71 E4
Ballycastle 69 E3
Ballyclare 71 E3
Ballyconneely 69 D2
Ballycotton 75 D2
Ballycumber 72 C3
Ballydehob 74 B1
Ballydesmond 74 C2
Ballyduff 74 B3
Ballyduff 75 E2
Ballyfarnan 70 B2
Ballygalley 71 F3
Ballygar 72 B4
Ballygawley 71 D2
Ballygowan 71 F2
Ballyhaise 71 D1
Ballyhale 73 D1
Ballyhaunis 70 B1
Ballyhean 69 E2
Ballyheige 74 B3
Ballyjamesduff 71 D1
Ballykeeran 72 C4
Ballylanders 75 D3
Ballylongford 74 C3
Ballylooby 72 B1
Ballylynan 73 D2
Ballymahon 72 C4
Ballymakeery 74 C2
Ballymaloe 75 D2
Ballymena 71 E3
Ballymoe 72 B4
Ballymoney 71 E4
Ballymore 72 C4
Ballymore Eustace 73 D3
Ballymote 70 B2
Ballynahinch 71 E2
Ballynure 71 E3
Ballyragget 72 C2
Ballyroan 72 C3
Ballyronan 71 E3
Ballysadare 70 B2
Ballyshannon 70 C2
Ballyvaughan 69 E1
Ballywalter 71 F2
Balrothery 73 E4
Baltimore 74 C1
Baltinglass 73 D2
Banagher 72 C3
Banbridge 71 E2
Bandon 75 D2
Bangor 71 F3
Bangor Erris 69 E3
Bansha 75 E3
Banteer 74 C2
Bantry 74 C1
Barryporeen 75 D3
Beaufort 74 B2
Belcoo 70 C2
Belfast 71 E3
Belgooly 75 D1
Bellaghy 71 E3
Belleek 70 C2
Belmullet (Béal an
Mhuirhead) 69 D3
Belturbet 70 C2
Benburb 71 D2
Bennettsbridge 73 D2
Beragh 71 D2
Birr 72 C3
Blacklion 70 C2
Blackwater 73 E1
Blarney 75 D2
Blessington 73 E3
Boherbue 74 C2
Borris 73 D2
Borris-in-Ossory 72 C3
Borrisokane 75 E4
Borrisoleigh 72 C2
Boyle 70 B1
Bracknagh 73 D3
Bray 73 E3
Bridgetown 73 D1
Brittas 73 E3
Broadford 75 D4
Broadford 74 C3
Broughshane 71 E3
Bruff 75 D3
Bruree 75 D3
Bunclody 73 D2

Buncrana 71 D4
Bundoran 70 B2
Bunmahon 72 C1
Bunnahowen 69 E3
Bunnyconnellan 69 F3
Bushmills 71 E4
Butler's Bridge 71 D1
Buttevant 75 D3

C

Cadarnstown 72 C3
Caherconlish 75 D3
Caherdaniel 74 B2
Cahersiveen 74 B2
Cahir 72 C1
Caledon 71 D2
Callan 72 C2
Caltra 72 B4
Camolin 73 E2
Camp 74 B3
Cappagh White 75 D3
Cappamore 75 D3
Cappoquin 72 C1
Carlanstown 71 D1
Carlingford 71 E1
Carlow 73 D2
Carndonagh 71 D4
Carnew 73 E2
Carnlough 71 E3
Carracastle 70 B1
Carrick (An Charraig)... 70 B3
Carrickfergus 71 F3
Carrickmacross 71 D1
Carrickmore 71 D3
Carrick-on-Shannon... 70 C1
Carrick-on-Suir 72 C1
Carrigahorig 72 B3
Carrigaline 75 D2
Carrigallen 70 C1
Carriganimmy 74 C2
Carrigans 71 D3
Carrigtohill 75 D2
Carrowkeel 71 D4
Carryduff 71 F2
Cashel 72 C2
Castlebar 69 E3
Castlebellingham 71 E1
Castleblayney 71 D2
Castlebridge 73 E1
Castlecomer 73 D2
Castle Cove 74 B2
Castlederg 70 C3
Castledermot 73 D2
Castleisland 74 C3
Castlemaine 74 B2
Castlemartyr 75 D2
Castleplunkett 70 B1
Castlepollard 73 D4
Castlerea 70 B1
Castlerock 71 D4
Castleshane 71 D2
Castletown 72 C2
Castletownbere 74 B1
Castletownroche 75 D2
Castletownshend 74 C1
Castlewellan 71 E2
Causeway 74 B3
Cavan 71 D1
Celbridge 73 E3
Charlestown 70 B1
Charleville
(Rath Luirc) 75 D3
Clady 70 C3
Clane 73 D3
Clara 72 C3
Clarecastle 74 C4
Claremorris 69 F2
Clarinbridge 72 A3
Clashmore 72 C1
Claudy 71 D3
Clifden 69 D2
Cliffony 70 B2
Clogh 73 D2
Cloghan 72 C3

Clogheen 72 B1
Clogher 71 D2
Clohamon 73 D2
Clonakilty 74 C1
Clonard 73 D4
Clonaslee 72 C3
Clonbulloge 73 D3
Clonbur
(An Fhairchel) 69 E2
Clondalkin 73 E3
Clones 71 D2
Clonmany 71 D4
Clonmel 72 C1
Clonmellon 73 D4
Clonmore 72 C2
Clonony 72 C3
Clonoulty 72 C2
Clonroche 73 D1
Clontibret 71 D2
Cloonbannin 74 C2
Cloondara 70 C1
Cloonkeen 74 C2
Cloonlara 75 D4
Clough 71 F2
Cloughjordan 72 C3
Cloyne 75 D2
Coagh 71 E3
Coalisland 71 D2
Cobh 75 D2
Coleraine 71 E4
Collinstown 73 D4
Collon 71 E1
Colloooney 70 B2
Comber 71 F2
Conna 75 D2
Cookstown 71 D3
Coole 72 C4
Cooraclare 74 C4
Cootehill 71 D2
Cork 75 D2
Cornamona 69 E2
Corofin 74 C4
Courtmacsherry 75 D1
Courtown Harbour 73 E2
Craigavon 71 E2
Craughwell 72 B3
Creggs 72 B4
Cresslough 70 C4
Croagh 74 C3
Crolly (Croithli) 70 B4
Crookedwood 73 D4
Crookhaven 74 B1
Crookstown 74 C2
Croom 75 D3
Crossakeel 73 D4
Cross Barry 75 D2
Crosshaven 75 D2
Crossmaglen 71 E1
Crossmolina 69 E3
Crumlin 71 E3
Crusheen 75 D4
Culdaff 71 D4
Culleybackey 71 E3
Curracloe 73 E1
Curraghboy 72 B4
Curry 70 B1
Cushendall 71 E4

D

Daingean 73 D3
Delvin 73 D4
Derrygonnelly 70 C2
Derrylin 70 C2
Dervock 71 E4
Dingle (An Daingean)... 74 B2
Doagh 71 E3
Donaghadee 71 F3
Donaghmore 72 C2
Donegal 70 C3
Doneraile 75 D2
Doonbeg 74 C4
Douglas 75 D2
Downpatrick 71 F2
Dowra 70 C2

Draperstown 71 D3
Drimoleague 74 C1
Dripsey 75 D2
Drogheda 73 E4
Dromahair 70 B2
Dromcolliher 74 C3
Dromore 71 E2
Dromore 70 C2
Dromore West 70 B2
Drum 71 D2
Drumconrath 70 D1
Drumkeeran 70 C2
Drumlish 70 C1
Drumod 70 C1
Drumquin 70 C3
Drumshanbo 70 C2
Drumsna 70 C1
Duagh 74 C3
Dublin 73 E3
Duleek 73 E4
Dunboyne 73 E3
Duncormick 73 D1
Dundalk 71 E1
Dunderrow 75 D1
Dundrum 71 F2
Dunfanaghy 70 C4
Dungannon 71 D2
Dungarvan 73 D2
Dungarvan 72 C1
Dungiven 71 D3
Dungloe 70 B3
Dungourney 75 D2
Dunkineely 70 B3
Dun Laoghaire 73 E3
Dunlavin 73 D3
Dunleer 71 E1
Dunloy 71 E3
Dunmanway 74 C2
Dunmore 72 B4
Dunmore East 73 D1
Dunmurry 71 E2
Dunshauglin 73 E4
Durrow 72 C2
Durras 74 B1

Frenchpark 70 B1
Freshford 72 C2
Fuerty 72 B4

Kanturk 74 C2
Keadue 70 C2
Keady 71 D2
Keel 69 D3
Keenagh 72 C4
Kells 71 E3
Kells 73 D4
Kenmare 74 B2
Kesh 70 C2
Kilbeggan 72 C3
Kilberry 73 D4
Kilbrittain 75 D1
Kilcar
  (Cill Charthaigh) 70 B3
Kilcock 73 D3
Kilcolgan 72 A3
Kilconnell 72 B3
Kilconnell 74 C4
Kilcoole 73 E3
Kilcormac 72 C3
Kilcullen 73 D3
Kilcurry 71 E1
Kildare 73 D3
Kildavin 73 D2
Kildorrery 75 D3
Kildress 71 D3
Kilfenora 74 C4
Kilfinnane 75 D3
Kilgarvan 74 C2
Kilkee 74 B4
Kilkeel 71 E1
Kilkelly 70 B1
Kilkenny 73 D2
Kilkieran
  (Cill Ciaráin) 69 E1
Kilkinlea 74 C3
Kill 72 C1
Killadysert 74 C3
Killala 69 E3
Killaloe 75 D4
Killarney 74 C2
Kilashandra 70 C1
Killashee 72 C4
Killeagh 72 B1
Killeigh 72 C3
Killenaule 72 C2
Killimer 74 C3
Killimor 72 B3
Killiney 73 E3
Killinick 73 E1
Killorglin 74 B2
Killough 71 F2
Killucan 73 D4
Killybegs 70 B3
Killyleagh 71 F2
Kilmaconoge 73 E3
Kilmacrenan 70 C4
Kilmacthomas 72 C1
Kilmaganny 72 C2
Kilmaine 69 E2
Kilmallock 75 D3
Kilmanagh 72 C2
Kilmanahan 72 C1
Kilmeaden 72 C1
Kilmeage 73 D3
Kilmedy 74 C3
Kilmichael 74 C2
Kilmore Quay 73 D1
Kilnaleck 71 D1
Kilrea 71 E3
Kilrush 74 C3
Kilsheelan 72 C1
Kiltealy 73 D2
Kiltegan 73 D2
Kiltimagh 70 A1
Kiltoom 72 C4
Kingscourt 71 D1
Kinlough 70 B2
Kinnegad 73 D4
Kinnitty 72 C3
Kinsale 75 D1
Kinvarra 69 F1
Kircubbin 71 F2
Knock 70 A1
Knockcroghery 72 C4

Knocklofty 72 C1
Knockmahon 72 C1
Knocktopher 73 D2

Lahinch 74 C4
Lanesborough 72 C4
Laragh 73 E3
Larne 71 F3
Lauragh 74 B2
Laurencetown 72 B3
Leap 74 C1
Leenane 69 E2
Leighlinbridge 73 D2
Leitrim 70 C1
Leixlip 73 E3
Lemybrien 72 C1
Letterfrack 69 D2
Letterkenny 70 C3
Lifford 70 C3
Limavady 71 D4
Limerick 75 D3
Lisbellaw 70 C2
Lisburn 71 E2
Liscarroll 75 D3
Lisdoonvarna 69 E1
Lismore 72 C1
Lisnaskea 70 C2
Lisryan 72 C4
Listowel 74 C3
Loghill 74 C3
Londonderry 71 D3
Longford 72 C4
Loughbrickland 71 E2
Loughgall 71 E2
Loughglinn 70 B1
Loughrea 72 B3
Louisburgh 69 E2
Lucan 73 E3
Lurgan 71 E2
Lusk 73 E4

K

L

E

Easky 70 A2
Edenderry 73 D3
Edgeworthstown 72 C4
Eglinton 71 D3
Elphin 70 B1
Emyvale 71 D2
Enfield 73 D3
Ennis 74 C4
Enniscorthy 73 D2
Enniscrone 69 F3
Enniskean 74 C2
Enniskillen 70 C2
Ennistymon 74 C4
Eyrecourt 72 B3

F

Farnaght 70 C1
Farranfore 74 B2
Feakle 75 D4
Fenagh 70 C1
Fermoy 75 D2
Ferns 73 E2
Fethard 72 C2
Fethard 73 D1
Finnea 70 C1
Fintona 71 D2
Fivemiletown 71 D2
Fontstown 73 D3
Foulksmills 73 D1
Foxford 69 F3
Foynes 74 C3
Freemount 74 C3

G

Galbally 75 D3
Galway 69 E1
Garrison 70 C2
Garristown 73 E4
Garvagh 71 D3
Geashill 72 C3
Gilford 71 E2
Glandore 74 C1
Glanworth 75 D2
Glaslough 71 D2
Glassan 72 C4
Glenamaddy 72 B4
Glenarm 71 E3
Glenavy 71 E3
Glenbeigh 74 B2
Glencolumbkille (Gleann
  Cholm Cille) 70 B3
Glendalough 73 E3
Glenealy 73 E2
Glenfarne 70 C2
Glengarriff 74 B2
Glenmore 73 D1
Glenties 70 B3
Glenville 75 D2
Glin 74 C3
Glinsk (Glinsce) 69 D2
Golden 72 C2
Goleen 74 B1
Goresbridge 73 D2
Gorey 73 E2
Gort 72 A3
Gortin 71 D3
Gowran 73 D2
Graiguenamanagh 73 D2
Grallagh 70 B1
Granard 70 C1
Grange 70 B2
Greencastle 71 E1
Greyabbey 71 F2
Greystones 73 E3
Gulladuff 71 E3

H

Hacketstown 73 D2
Headford 69 E2
Herbertstown 75 D2
Hillsborough 71 E2
Hilltown 71 E2
Hospital 75 D3
Holycross 72 C2
Holywood 71 F3
Howth 73 E3

I

Inch 74 B2
Inchigeelagh 74 C2
Inishannon 75 D2
Irvinestown 70 C2

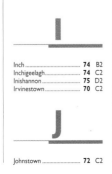

J

Johnstown 72 C2

M

Macroom 74 C2
Maghera 71 D3
Maghera 71 E2
Magherafelt 71 E3
Maguiresbridge 70 C2
Malahide 73 E3
Malin 71 D4
Malin More 70 B3
Mallow 75 D2
Manorhamilton 70 C2
Markethill 71 E2
Maynooth 73 D3
Maze 71 E2
Middletown 71 D2
Midleton 75 D2
Milford 70 C4
Millstreet 74 C2
Milltown 74 B2
Milltown Malbay 74 C4
Mitchelstown 75 D3
Moate 72 C3
Mohill 70 C1
Molls Gap 74 B2
Monaghan 71 D2
Monasterevin 73 D3
Moneygall 72 C4
Moneymore 71 D3
Monivea 72 B3
Mooncoin 72 C1
Moorfields 71 E3
Mount Bellew 72 B4
Mount Charles 70 C3
Mountmellick 72 C3
Mountrath 72 C3
Mountshannon 75 D4

Mourne Abbey............. 75 D2
Moville......................... 71 D4
Moy.............................. 71 D2
Moylett......................... 71 D1
Moynalty...................... 71 D1
Moyvore....................... 72 C4
Muckross..................... 74 C2
Muff............................. 71 D4
Mullabohy.................... 71 E1
Mullagh........................ 73 D4
Mullinavat.................... 73 D1
Mullingar..................... 73 D4
Myshall........................ 73 D2

Naas............................ 73 D3
Nad............................. 74 C2
Naul............................ 73 E4
Navan.......................... 73 D4
Neale........................... 69 E2
Nenagh........................ 75 D4
Newbliss...................... 71 D2
Newbridge
(Droichead Nua)......... 73 D3
Newcastle.................... 71 E2
Newcastle West........... 74 C3
Newinn........................ 72 C2
Newmarket.................. 74 C3
Newmarket-
on-Fergus................... 74 C4
Newport...................... 69 E3
Newport...................... 75 D3
New Ross..................... 73 D1
Newry.......................... 71 E2
Newtown..................... 73 D2
Newtownabbey............. 71 E3
Newtownards................ 71 F3
Newtownhamilton......... 71 E2
Newtownmount-
kennedy...................... 73 E3
Newtownstewart........... 71 D3
Newtown Butler........... 71 D2
Newtown Forbes.......... 70 C1
Nobber........................ 71 D1

Oilgate......................... 73 D1
Oldcastle..................... 71 D1
Omagh......................... 71 D3
Omeath........................ 71 E1
Oola............................ 75 D3
Oranmore.................... 69 F1
Oughterard.................. 69 E2
Ovens.......................... 75 D2

Pallas Grean................ 75 D3
Parknasilla................... 74 B2
Partry.......................... 69 E2
Passage East................ 73 D1
Passage West............... 75 D2
Patrickswell................. 75 D3
Paulstown.................... 73 D2
Pettigo........................ 70 C3
Plumbridge.................. 71 D3
Pomeroy...................... 71 D3
Portadown................... 71 E2
Portaferry.................... 71 F2
Portarlington............... 73 D3
Portavogie................... 71 F2
Portglenone................ 71 E3
Portlaoise................... 73 D3
Portmarnock................ 73 E3
Portrane...................... 73 E4
Portroe....................... 75 D4
Portrush...................... 71 E4
Portstewart................. 71 D4
Portumna..................... 72 B3
Poyntzpass.................. 71 E2

Raharney...................... 73 D4
Randalstown................ 71 E3
Rasharkin..................... 71 E3
Rathangen................... 73 D3
Rathcoole.................... 73 E3
Rathcormack................ 75 D2
Rathdowney................. 72 C2
Rathdrum.................... 73 E2
Rathfriland................... 71 E2
Rathkeale.................... 74 C3
Rathmelton.................. 70 C4
Rathmolyon................. 73 D4
Rathmore..................... 74 C2
Rathmullan.................. 70 C4
Rathnew...................... 73 E3
Rathowen..................... 72 C4
Rathvilty...................... 73 D2
Ratoath....................... 73 E4
Ray............................. 70 C4
Ring (An Rinn)............. 72 C1
Ringaskiddy................. 75 D2
Riverstown.................. 72 C3
Rockcorry.................... 71 D2
Roosky........................ 70 C1
Rosapenna................... 70 C4
Rosbercon................... 73 D1
Roscommon................. 72 B4
Roscrea....................... 72 C3
Ross Carbery............... 74 C1
Rosscor....................... 70 C2
Rosses Point............... 70 B2
Rosslare Harbour........ 73 E1
Rosslea....................... 71 D2
Rostrevor.................... 71 E2
Roundstone................. 69 D2
Roundwood................. 73 E3
Rush........................... 73 E4

St Johnstown............... 70 C3
Saintfield.................... 71 F2
Sallins........................ 73 D3
Scarriff....................... 75 D4
Scartaglen................... 74 C2
Scarva........................ 71 E2
Schull......................... 74 B1
Scramoge.................... 70 C1
Scribbagh.................... 70 C2
Seskinore.................... 71 D2
Shanagolden............... 74 C3
Shannonbridge............ 72 C3
Shercock.................... 71 D1
Shillelagh.................... 73 E2
Shinrone..................... 72 C3
Shrule........................ 69 E2
Silvermines................. 75 D4
Sion Mills................... 70 C3
Sixmilebridge.............. 75 D4
Skerries...................... 73 E4
Skibbereen.................. 74 C1
Slane.......................... 73 E4
Sligo.......................... 70 B2
Smithborough............. 71 D2
Sneem........................ 74 B2
Spiddal (An Spideal).... 69 E1
Stewartstown.............. 71 D3
Stonyford................... 73 D2
Strabane..................... 70 C3
Stradbally................... 73 D3
Stradone..................... 71 D1
Strandhill................... 70 B2
Strangford.................. 71 F2
Stranorlar................... 70 C3
Stratford.................... 73 D3
Strokestown............... 70 C1
Summerhill................. 73 D4
Swanlinbar.................. 70 C2
Swatragh.................... 71 D3
Swinford..................... 70 A1
Swords....................... 73 E4

Tinahely...................... 73 E2
Tipperary.................... 75 D3
Tobercurry.................. 70 B2
Tobermore.................. 71 D3
Togher....................... 72 C3
Toomyvara.................. 72 B2
Toormoore.................. 74 B1
Tralee......................... 74 B3
Tramore..................... 73 D1
Trim........................... 73 D4
Tuam.......................... 72 B4
Tuamgraney................ 75 D4
Tulla.......................... 75 D4
Tullamore................... 72 C3
Tullow........................ 73 D2
Tulsk.......................... 70 B1
Turlough..................... 69 E3
Tyholland................... 71 D2
Tyrrellspass................ 72 C3

Urlingford................... 72 C2

Virginia...................... 71 D1

Waddington................ 73 D1
Warrenpoint............... 71 E2
Waterford.................. 73 D1
Watergrasshill............ 75 D2
Waterville................... 74 B2
Westport.................... 69 E2
Wexford..................... 73 E1
Whitegate.................. 75 D2
Whitehead.................. 71 F3
Wicklow..................... 73 E2
Woodenbridge............ 73 E2
Woodford................... 72 B3

Taghmon..................... 73 D1
Tagoat........................ 73 E1
Tahilla........................ 74 B2
Tallaght...................... 73 E3
Tallow........................ 72 B1
Tallowbridge............... 72 B1
Tandragee................... 71 E2
Tang.......................... 72 C4
Tarbert....................... 74 C3
Templemore................ 72 C2
Templepatrick............. 71 E3
Templetouhy............... 72 C2
Termonfeckin.............. 73 E4
Thomas Street............ 72 B4
Thomastown............... 73 D2
Thurles...................... 72 C2
Timahoe..................... 73 D3
Timoleague................. 74 C1

Youghal....................... 75 E2

Abberley 23 SO76
Abbey Town 43 NY15
Abbot's Salford 24 SP05
Abbots Bromley 31 SK02
Abbotsbury 9 SY58
Aberaeron 21 SN46
Aberarth 21 SN46
Aberchirder 62 NJ65
Abercraf 22 SN81
Aberdare 14 SO00
Aberdaron 28 SH12
Aberdeen 57 NJ90
Aberdour 48 NT18
Aberdyfi 22 SN69
Aberfeldy 52 NN84
Aberffraw 28 SH36
Aberford 36 SE43
Aberfoyle 52 NN50
Abergavenny 23 SO21
Abergele 29 SH97
Aberlady 48 NT47
Aberlour 61 NJ24
Abernethy 53 NO11
Aberporth 20 SN25
Abersoch 28 SH32
Abersychan 14 SO20
Abertillery 14 SO20
Aberystwyth 22 SN58
Abingdon 16 SU49
Abington 47 NS92
Aboyne 57 NO59
Abridge 18 TQ49
Accrington 35 SD72
Acharacle 54 NM66
Achiltibuie 64 NC00
Achnacroish 54 NM84
Achnamara 51 NR78
Achnasheen 59 NH15
Acle 27 TG41
Adderbury 24 SP43
Addington 12 TQ65
Adlington 34 SD61
Ainsdale 34 SD31
Aintree 34 SJ39
Aird Uig 64 NB03
Airdrie 47 NS76
Airth 52 NS98
Aith 63 HU35
Albrighton(Wolverhampton) .. 23 SJ80
Alcester 24 SP05
Alconbury 25 TL17
Aldbrough 37 TA23
Aldeburgh 19 TM45
Alderley Edge 30 SJ87
Aldermaston 16 SU56
Alderminster 24 SP24
Aldershot 11 SU85
Aldridge 24 SK00
Aldwark 40 SE46
Alexandria 51 NS37
Alford 57 NJ51
Alford 33 TF47
Alfreton 31 SK45
Alfriston 12 TQ50
Allendale 44 NY85
Allerton 35 SE13
Allesley 24 SP38
Allhallows-on-Sea 13 TQ87
Alloa 52 NS89
Allonby 43 NY04
Alloway 47 NS31
Almondsbury 15 ST68
Alness 60 NH66
Alnmouth 45 NU21
Alnwick 49 NU11
Alperton 17 TQ18
Alrewas 31 SK11
Alsager 30 SJ75
Alston 44 NY74
Altarnun 5 SX28
Altham 35 SD73
Althorpe 36 SE80
Altnaharra 66 NC53
Alton 11 SU73
Alton 31 SK04
Altrincham 35 SJ78
Alva 52 NS89
Alvechurch 24 SP07
Alveley 23 SO78
Alveston 15 ST68
Alwalton 25 TL19

Alyth 53 NO24
Amberley 15 SO80
Amberley 11 TQ01
Amble 45 NU20
Amblecote 23 SO88
Ambleside 39 NY30
Amersham 17 SU99
Amesbury 10 SU14
Amlwch 28 SH49
Ammanford 21 SN61
Ampfield 10 SU42
Ampleforth 40 SE67
Ampthill 25 TL03
Ancaster 32 SK94
Ancroft 49 NT94
Ancrum 48 NT62
Andover 10 SU34
Andoversford 24 SP01
Andreas 38 SC49
Angle 20 SM80
Annan 43 NY16
Annfield Plain 45 NZ15
Anstey 24 SK50
Anstruther 53 NO50
Ansty 24 SP48
Appleby-in-Westmorland 39 NY62
Applecross 59 NG74
Appledore 6 SS43
Appleton-le-Moors 41 SE78
Arbroath 53 NO64
Archiestown 61 NJ24
Archirondel 9 JS00
Ardarroch 59 NG83
Ardbeg 50 NR44
Ardelve 59 NG82
Arden 51 NS38
Ardentinny 51 NS18
Ardersier 61 NH75
Ardfern 51 NM80
Ardgour 55 NN06
Ardingly 12 TQ32
Ardleigh 19 TM02
Ardlui 51 NN31
Ardlussa 50 NR68
Ardrishaig 51 NR88
Ardrossan 46 NS24
Arduaine 51 NM71
Ardvasar 54 NG60
Ardwell 42 NX14
Arinagour 50 NM25
Arisaig 54 NM68
Armadale 47 NS96
Armathwaite 44 NY54
Arncliffe 39 SD97
Arnprior 52 NS69
Arnside 39 SD47
Arrochar 51 NN20
Arundel 11 TQ00
Ascog 51 NS16
Ascot 17 SU96
Ash 13 TR25
Ash 11 SU95
Ashbourne 31 SK14
Ashburton 8 SX77
Ashbury 16 SU28
Ashby Parva 24 SP58
Ashby-de-la-Zouch 31 SK31
Ashford 13 TR04
Ashford 17 TQ07
Ashford in the Water 31 SK16
Ashington 45 NZ28
Ashington 11 TQ11
Ashtead 17 TQ15
Ashton-in-Makerfield 34 SJ59
Ashton-under-Lyne 35 SJ99
Ashurst 10 SU31
Askam in Furness 38 SD27
Askern 36 SE51
Askrigg 39 SD99
Aspatria 43 NY14
Aspley Guise 25 SP93
Aspull 34 SD60
Aston Clinton 16 SP81
Aston on Clun 23 SO38
Atherstone 24 SP39
Atherton 34 SD60
Attleborough 27 TM09
Auchencairn 43 NX75
Auchterarder 52 NN91
Auchterderran 53 NT29
Auchterhouse 53 NO33
Auchterless 62 NJ74
Auchtermuchty 53 NO21
Auchtertyre 59 NG82
Audenshaw 35 SJ99
Audlem 30 SJ64
Aughton 34 SD30

Auldearn 61 NH95
Auldgirth 43 NX98
Aultbea 59 NG88
Austwick 39 SD76
Avebury 15 SU16
Aviemore 56 NH81
Avonbridge 47 NS97
Avonmouth 14 ST57
Axbridge 14 ST45
Axminster 8 SY29
Aylesbury 16 SP81
Aylesford 12 TQ75
Aylsham 27 TG12
Aynho 24 SP53
Ayr 47 NS32
Aysgarth 40 SE08
Ayton 49 NT96

Babbacombe 8 SX96
Backaland 67 HY53
Bacton 27 TG33
Bacup 35 SD82
Bagby 40 SE48
Bagh a Chaisteil 64 NL69
Bagillt 29 SJ27
Bagshot 16 SU96
Baile a Mhanaich 64 NF75
Baile Ailein 64 NB22
Baillieston 47 NS66
Bainbridge 39 SD99
Bainton 36 SE95
Bakewell 31 SK26
Bala 29 SH93
Balallan 64 NB22
Balbeggie 53 NO12
Balblair 60 NH76
Baldersby 40 SE37
Balderton 32 SK85
Baldock 18 TL23
Baldrine 38 SC48
Balfour 67 HY41
Balfron 52 NS58
Balintore 61 NH87
Balivanich 64 NF75
Ballachulish 55 NN05
Ballantrae 42 NX08
Ballasalla 38 SC27
Ballater 57 NO39
Ballaugh 38 SC39
Ballinluig 52 NN95
Ballintuim 52 NO15
Balloch 51 NS38
Ballygrant 50 NR36
Balmacara 59 NG82
Balmaha 51 NS49
Balmedie 57 NJ91
Balquhidder 52 NN52
Balsall Common 24 SP27
Balsham 18 TL55
Baltasound 63 HP60
Bamber Bridge 34 SD52
Bamburgh 49 NU13
Bamford 31 SK28
Bampton 39 NY51
Bampton 7 SS92
Bampton 16 SP30
Banavie 55 NN17
Banbury 24 SP44
Banchory 57 NO69
Banff 62 NJ66
Bangor 28 SH57
Bangor-is-y-coed 30 SJ34
Bankfoot 52 NO03
Banks 34 SD32
Bannockburn 52 NS89
Banstead 12 TQ25
Banwell 14 ST35
Bar Hill 18 TL36
Barabhas 64 NB34
Barbon 39 SD68
Bardney 33 TF16
Bardon Mill 44 NY76
Bardsea 38 SD37
Barford 24 SP26
Barford St. Martin 15 SU03
Bargoed 14 ST19
Bargrennan 42 NX37
Barham 13 TR25
Barking 18 TQ48
Barkingside 18 TQ48

Place	Page	Grid
Barlby	36	SE63
Barley	18	TL43
Barmby Moor	36	SE74
Barmouth	28	SH61
Barnard Castle	40	NZ01
Barnby Moor	32	SK68
Barnet	17	TQ29
Barnham Broom	27	TG00
Barnoldswick	35	SD84
Barnsdale Bar	36	SE51
Barnsley	35	SE30
Barnstaple	6	SS53
Barnton	48	NT17
Barr	42	NX29
Barrhead	47	NS45
Barrhill	42	NX28
Barrow-in-Furness	38	SD26
Barry	7	ST16
Barry Island	7	ST16
Barton	18	TL45
Barton	34	SD53
Barton Mills	26	TL77
Barton on Sea	10	SZ29
Barton Stacey	10	SU44
Barton-le-Clay	25	TL03
Barton-under-Needwood	31	SK11
Barton-Upon-Humber	37	TA02
Barvas	64	NB34
Basildon	18	TQ78
Basingstoke	11	SU65
Baslow	31	SK27
Bassenthwaite	44	NY23
Baston	33	TF11
Bath	15	ST76
Bathgate	48	NS96
Batley	35	SE22
Battle	12	TQ71
Baughurst	16	SU56
Baumber	33	TF27
Bawdeswell	27	TG02
Bawtry	36	SK69
Baycliff	38	SD27
Baydon	16	SU27
Beachley	14	ST59
Beaconsfield	17	SU99
Beadnell	49	NU22
Beaminster	9	ST40
Beamish	45	NZ25
Bearsden	47	NS57
Beattock	43	NT00
Beaulieu	10	SU30
Beauly	60	NH54
Beaumaris	28	SH67
Beaumont	9	JS00
Bebington	29	SJ38
Beccles	27	TM48
Beckenham	17	TQ36
Beckhampton	15	SU06
Beckington	15	ST85
Becquet Vincent	9	JS00
Bedale	40	SE28
Beddgelert	28	SH54
Beddingham	12	TQ40
Bedford	25	TL04
Bedlington	45	NZ28
Bedlinog	14	SO00
Bedwas	14	ST18
Bedworth	37	SP38
Beeford	37	TA15
Beer	8	SY28
Beeston	30	SJ55
Beeston	32	SK53
Beetham	39	SD47
Beetley	27	TF91
Beith	47	NS35
Belbroughton	24	SO97
Belford	49	NU13
Bellingham	44	NY88
Bellochantuy	46	NR63
Bellshill	47	NS76
Belmont	34	SD61
Belmont	63	HP50
Belper	31	SK34
Belsay	45	NZ07
Belton	36	SE70
Belton	32	SK93
Bembridge	11	SZ68
Benderloch	54	NM93
Benllech	28	SH58
Benson	16	SU69
Bentley	36	SE50
Benwick	26	TL39
Bere Alston	5	SX46
Bere Ferrers	5	SX46
Bere Regis	9	SY89
Berkeley	15	ST69
Berkeley Road	15	SO70
Berkhamsted	17	SP90
Bernisdale	58	NG45
Berriedale	67	ND12
Berriew	22	SJ10
Berrow	14	ST25
Berrynarbor	6	SS54
Berwick	12	TQ50
Berwick-upon-Tweed	49	NT95
Bethersden	13	TQ94
Bethesda	28	SH66
Bettyhill	66	NC76
Betws-y-coed	29	SH75
Beulah	22	SN95
Beverley	37	TA03
Bewdley	23	SO77
Bexhill	12	TQ70
Bexley	12	TQ47
Bexleyheath	12	TQ47
Bibury	15	SP10
Bicester	16	SP52
Bickleigh	6	SS90
Biddenden	13	TQ83
Biddulph	30	SJ85
Bideford	6	SS42
Bidford-on-Avon	24	SP15
Bigbury-on-Sea	5	SX64
Biggar	38	SD16
Biggar	48	NT03
Biggin Hill	12	TQ45
Biggleswade	25	TL14
Bilbrook	7	ST04
Bilbrough	36	SE54
Bildeston	19	TL94
Billericay	18	TQ69
Billinge	34	SD50
Billingham	40	NZ42
Billingshurst	11	TQ02
Billington	35	SD73
Bilston	24	SO99
Binbrook	37	TF29
Bingham	32	SK73
Bingley	35	SE13
Birchgrove	21	SS79
Birchington	13	TR36
Birdlip	24	SO91
Birkenhead	34	SJ38
Birmingham	24	SP08
Birstall	35	SE22
Bishop Auckland	40	NZ22
Bishop's Castle	23	SO38
Bishop's Frome	23	SO64
Bishop's Stortford	18	TL42
Bishop's Tawton	6	SS52
Bishop's Waltham	10	SU51
Bishopbriggs	47	NS67
Bishops Lydeard	14	ST12
Bishopsteignton	8	SX97
Bishopton	51	NS47
Blaby	24	SP59
Black Torrington	6	SS40
Blackburn	34	SD62
Blackburn	48	NS96
Blackford	52	NN80
Blackmill	21	SS98
Blackpool	34	SD33
Blackrod	34	SD61
Blackwater	10	SZ58
Blackwaterfoot	46	NR92
Blackwood	14	ST19
Blaenau Ffestiniog	28	SH74
Blaenavon	14	SO20
Blaengarw	21	SS99
Blagdon	14	ST55
Blair Atholl	56	NN86
Blairgowrie	53	NO14
Blakeney	15	SO60
Blakeney	27	TG04
Blanchland	45	NY95
Blandford Forum	9	ST80
Blawith	38	SD28
Blaxton	36	SE60
Blaydon	45	NZ16
Bleddfa	22	SO26
Bletchley	25	SP83
Blickling	27	TG12
Blidworth	31	SK55
Blockley	24	SP13
Bloxham	24	SP43
Blubberhouses	40	SE15
Blue Anchor	7	ST04
Blundellsands	34	SJ39
Blyth	32	SK68
Blyth	45	NZ38
Blyton	36	SK89
Bo'Ness	48	NT08
Boat of Garten	56	NH91
Boddam	63	NK14
Boddam	63	HU31
Bodelwyddan	29	SJ07
Bodfari	29	SJ07
Bodinnick	5	SX15
Bodmin	5	SX06
Bognor Regis	11	SZ99
Boldon	45	NZ36
Bollington	31	SJ97
Bolney	12	TQ22
Bolsover	32	SK47
Bolton	34	SD70
Bolton Abbey	35	SE05
Bolton Bridge	35	SE05
Bolton le Sands	39	SD46
Bonar Bridge	66	NH69
Bonchester Bridge	44	NT51
Bonnybridge	52	NS87
Bonnyrigg	48	NT36
Bontddu	28	SH61
Bonvilston	14	ST07
Boot	38	NY10
Bootle	38	SD18
Bootle	34	SJ39
Bordeaux	34	GN00
Bordon	11	SU83
Boreham Street	12	TQ61
Borehamwood	17	TQ19
Borgue	43	NX64
Borgue	67	ND12
Borough Green	12	TQ65
Boroughbridge	40	SE36
Borrowdale	38	NY21
Borth	22	SN69
Boscastle	5	SX09
Bosham	11	SU80
Boston	33	TF34
Botesdale	27	TM07
Bothel	43	NY13
Bothwell	47	NS75
Botley	10	SU51
Bottesford	32	SK83
Bottisham	18	TL56
Boughton Monchelsea	12	TQ74
Boughton Street	13	TR05
Bourne	33	TF02
Bourne End	16	SU88
Bournemouth	10	SZ09
Bourton-on-the-Water	24	SP12
Bovey Tracey	8	SX87
Bovingdon	17	TL00
Bowes	39	NY91
Bowmore	50	NR35
Bowness-on-Windermere	39	SD49
Box	15	ST86
Bozeat	25	SP95
Bracklesham	11	SZ89
Brackley	25	SP53
Bracknell	16	SU86
Braco	52	NN80
Bradford	35	SE13
Bradford-on-Avon	15	ST86
Brading	10	SZ68
Bradwell	31	SK18
Bradwell-on-Sea	19	TM00
Bradworthy	6	SS31
Brae	63	HU36
Braemar	56	NO19
Braintree	18	TL72
Braithwaite	38	NY22
Braithwell	36	SK59
Bramber	11	TQ11
Bramhall	30	SJ88
Bramhope	35	SE24
Bramley	16	SK47
Bramley	16	SU65
Brampton	25	TL27
Brampton	44	NY56
Brancaster	26	TF74
Brancepeth	45	NZ23
Brandesburton	37	TA14
Brandon	26	TL78
Brandon	24	SP47
Bransome	10	SZ09
Bransford	23	SO75
Branston	32	TF06
Bratton Clovelly	5	SX49
Bratton Fleming	6	SS63
Braunton	6	SS43
Bray	16	SU97
Brayford	6	SS63
Breadsall	31	SK33
Bream	15	SO60
Brean	14	ST25
Breascleit	64	NB23
Breasclete	64	NB23
Brechfa	21	SN53
Brechin	57	NO66

Brecon 22 SO02
Bredhurst 12 TQ76
Bredon 24 SO93
Bredwardine 23 SO34
Brendon 7 SS74
Brentford 17 TQ17
Brentwood 18 TQ59
Brenzett 13 TR02
Bretby 31 SK22
Bride 38 NX40
Bridge of Allan 52 NS79
Bridge of Balgie 52 NN54
Bridge of Cally 53 NO15
Bridge of Don 57 NJ90
Bridge of Earn 52 NO11
Bridge of Marnoch 62 NJ55
Bridge of Orchy 55 NN23
Bridge of Weir 51 NS36
Bridgend 21 SS97
Bridgend 50 NR36
Bridgnorth 23 SO79
Bridgwater 14 ST23
Bridlington 41 TA16
Bridport 9 SY49
Brierfield 35 SD83
Brierley Hill 24 SO98
Brigg 37 TA00
Brighouse 35 SE12
Brighstone 10 SZ48
Brighton 12 TQ30
Brimington 31 SK47
Brinklow 24 SP47
Brinyan 67 HY42
Brislington 15 ST67
Bristol 15 ST57
Briton Ferry 21 SS79
Brixham 8 SX95
Brixworth 25 SP77
Broad Haven 20 SM81
Broadford 58 NG62
Broadstairs 13 TR36
Broadway 24 SP03
Broadwindsor 9 ST40
Brockenhurst 10 SU30
Brodick 46 NS03
Bromborough 30 SJ38
Brome 27 TM17
Bromham 25 TL05
Bromley 12 TQ46
Bromsgrove 24 SO97
Bromyard 23 SO65
Brook 10 SU21
Brooke 27 TM29
Broomhill 45 NU20
Brora 66 NC90
Brotton 41 NZ61
Brough 39 NY71
Broughton 48 NT13
Broughton 34 SD53
Broughton-in-Furness 38 SD28
Broughty Ferry 53 NO43
Brownhills 31 SK00
Broxbourne 17 TL30
Broxburn 48 NT07
Broxted 18 TL52
Broxton 30 SJ45
Bruichladdich 50 NR26
Bruton 15 ST63
Bryn 34 SD50
Brynaman 21 SN71
Brynmawr 14 SO11
Bubwith 36 SE73
Buchlyvie 52 NS59
Buckden 25 TL16
Buckden 39 SD97
Buckfastleigh 8 SX76
Buckhaven 53 NT39
Buckhurst Hill 18 TQ49
Buckie 62 NJ46
Buckingham 25 SP63
Buckland 24 SP03
Buckland Newton 9 ST60
Bucklers Hard 10 SU40
Buckley 29 SJ26
Bucklow Hill 30 SJ78
Bude 6 SS20
Budleigh Salterton 8 SY08
Budock Water 4 SW73
Bugbrooke 25 SP65
Builth Wells 22 SO05
Bulkington 24 SP38
Bulphan 18 TQ68
Bunessan 54 NM32
Bungay 27 TM38
Buntingford 17 TL32
Bunwell 27 TM19
Burbage 15 SU26

Bures 19 TL93
Burford 16 SP21
Burgess Hill 12 TQ31
Burgh by Sands 44 NY35
Burgh Heath 12 TQ25
Burghead 61 NJ16
Burlescombe 7 ST01
Burley 10 SU20
Burley in Wharfedale 35 SE14
Burleydam 30 SJ64
Burlton 30 SJ42
Burnham 17 SU98
Burnham Market 26 TF84
Burnham-on-Crouch 19 TQ99
Burnham-on-Sea 14 ST34
Burnley 35 SD83
Burnopfield 45 NZ15
Burnsall 40 SE06
Burnt Yates 40 SE26
Burntisland 48 NT28
Burntwood 31 SK00
Burrafirth 63 HP61
Burravoe 63 HU58
Burrelton 53 NO23
Burrington 6 SS61
Burry Port 21 SN40
Burscough 34 SD41
Burscough Bridge 34 SD41
Burslem 30 SJ84
Burton Agnes 41 TA16
Burton Bradstock 9 SY48
Burton Latimer 25 SP97
Burton upon Stather 36 SE81
Burton upon Trent 31 SK22
Burwash 12 TQ62
Burwell 18 TL56
Burwick 67 ND48
Bury 35 SD81
Bury St. Edmunds 19 TL86
Bushey 17 TQ19
Butley 19 TM35
Buttermere 38 NY11
Buxton 31 SK07
Bwlch 22 SO12
Byfleet 17 TQ06
Bylchau 29 SH96

C

Cadnam 10 SU31
Caergwrle 29 SJ35
Caerleon 14 ST39
Caernarfon 28 SH46
Caerphilly 14 ST18
Caersws 22 SO09
Caerwent 14 ST49
Cairndow 51 NN11
Cairnryan 42 NX06
Caister-on-Sea 27 TG51
Caistor 37 TA10
Calbourne 10 SZ48
Caldbeck 44 NY34
Calder Bridge 38 NY00
Calderbrook 35 SD91
Caldercruix 47 NS86
Caldicot 14 ST48
Calfsound 67 HY53
Calgary 54 NM35
Callander 52 NN60
Callington 5 SX36
Calne 15 ST97
Calvine 56 NN86
Camber 13 TQ91
Camberley 16 SU86
Camborne 4 SW64
Cambridge 18 TL45
Cambusbarron 52 NS79
Cambuslang 47 NS66
Camelford 5 SX18
Campbeltown 46 NR72
Candlesby 33 TF46
Canford Cliffs 10 SZ08
Cannich 60 NH33
Cannock 31 SJ91
Canonbie 44 NY37
Canterbury 13 TR15
Canvey Island 18 TQ78
Caoles 50 NM04
Capel 11 TQ14
Capel Curig 28 SH75
Caputh 52 NO04
Carbis Bay 4 SW53

Carbost 58 NG33
Carcroft 36 SE50
Cardiff 14 ST17
Cardigan 20 SN14
Cardross 51 NS37
Carfraemill 48 NT55
Carisbrooke 10 SZ48
Cark 39 SD37
Carlabhagh 64 NB24
Carlisle 44 NY35
Carloway 64 NB24
Carlton 40 SE08
Carluke 47 NS85
Carlyon Bay 5 SX05
Carmarthen 21 SN42
Carnforth 39 SD47
Carnoustie 53 NO53
Carnwath 48 NS94
Carperby 40 SE08
Carradale 46 NR83
Carrbridge 61 NH92
Carrefour 9 JS00
Carrutherstown 43 NY17
Carrville 45 NZ34
Carsphairn 42 NX59
Carstairs 47 NS94
Carterton 16 SP20
Cartmel 39 SD37
Casterton 39 SD67
Castle Ashby 25 SP85
Castle Bromwich 24 SP18
Castle Cary 15 ST63
Castle Combe 15 ST87
Castle Donington 31 SK42
Castle Douglas 43 NX76
Castle Rising 26 TF62
Castlebay 64 NL69
Castleford 36 SE42
Castlemartin 20 SR99
Castleside 45 NZ04
Castleton 31 SK18
Castleton 41 NZ60
Castletown 67 ND16
Castletown 38 SC26
Catel 9 GN00
Caterham 12 TQ35
Catterick Bridge 40 SE29
Cavendish 18 TL84
Caversham 16 SU77
Cawdor 61 NH85
Cawood 36 SE53
Caxton 18 TL35
Cemaes 28 SH39
Cemmaes Road 22 SH80
Cerne Abbas 9 ST60
Cerrigydrudion 29 SH94
Chacewater 4 SW74
Chadderton 35 SD90
Chaddesley Corbett 23 SO87
Chadlington 16 SP32
Chadwell Heath 12 TQ48
Chagford 8 SX78
Chale 10 SZ47
Chalfont St. Peter 17 TQ09
Chalford 15 SO80
Challock Lees 13 TR05
Chandler's Ford 10 SU41
Chapel St. Leonards 33 TF57
Chapel-en-le-Frith 31 SK08
Chapelton 47 NS64
Chapeltown 36 SK39
Chard 8 ST30
Chardstock 8 ST30
Charing 13 TQ94
Charingworth 24 SP13
Charlbury 16 SP31
Charlecote 24 SP25
Charlesworth 35 SK09
Charlton Marshall 9 ST90
Charlwood 11 TQ24
Charmouth 9 SY39
Charnock Richard 34 SD51
Chatham 12 TQ76
Chatteris 26 TL38
Chatton 49 NU02
Chawleigh 6 SS71
Cheadle 35 SJ88
Cheadle 31 SK04
Cheadle Hulme 30 SJ88
Cheam 12 TQ26
Cheddar 14 ST45
Chelford 30 SJ87
Chelmsford 18 TL70
Cheltenham 24 SO92
Chelwood 15 ST66
Chelwood Gate 12 TQ43
Chenies 17 TQ09

Chepstow ... 14 ST59
Cheriton Bishop ... 8 SX79
Cheriton Fitzpaine ... 7 SS80
Chertsey ... 17 TQ06
Chesham ... 17 SP90
Cheshunt ... 17 TL30
Chessington ... 17 TQ16
Chester ... 30 SJ46
Chester-le-Street ... 45 NZ25
Chesterfield ... 31 SK37
Chesterton ... 30 SJ84
Chichester ... 11 SU80
Chiddingfold ... 11 SU93
Chigwell ... 18 TQ49
Chilcompton ... 15 ST65
Childer Thornton ... 30 SJ37
Chillington ... 8 SX74
Chilmark ... 15 ST93
Chilwell ... 32 SK53
Chingford ... 18 TQ39
Chinnor ... 16 SP70
Chippenham ... 15 ST97
Chipperfield ... 17 TL00
Chipping ... 34 SD64
Chipping Campden ... 24 SP13
Chipping Norton ... 24 SP32
Chipping Ongar ... 18 TL50
Chirbury ... 23 SO29
Chirk ... 29 SJ23
Chirnside ... 49 NT85
Chittlehamholt ... 6 SS62
Chobham ... 17 SU96
Cholderton ... 10 SU24
Chollerford ... 45 NY97
Chorley ... 34 SD51
Chorleywood ... 17 TQ09
Christchurch ... 10 SZ19
Chudleigh ... 8 SX87
Chudleigh Knighton ... 8 SX87
Chulmleigh ... 6 SS61
Church Stoke ... 23 SO29
Church Stretton ... 23 SO49
Churston Ferrers ... 8 SX95
Churt ... 11 SU83
Cinderford ... 23 SO61
Cirencester ... 15 SP00
Clachan ... 58 NG53
Clachan ... 46 NR75
Clachan-Seil ... 51 NM71
Clacton-on-Sea ... 19 TM11
Cladich ... 51 NN02
Clanfield ... 16 SP20
Claonaig ... 46 NR85
Clapham ... 25 TL05
Clapham ... 39 SD76
Clare ... 18 TL74
Claverdon ... 24 SP16
Clavering ... 18 TL43
Clawton ... 6 SX39
Clayton-le-Moors ... 35 SD73
Clearwell ... 14 SO50
Cleator ... 38 NY01
Cleator Moor ... 38 NY01
Cleckheaton ... 35 SE12
Cleethorpes ... 37 TA30
Cleeve ... 14 ST46
Cleeve Hill ... 24 SO92
Cleish ... 52 NT09
Cleland ... 47 NS75
Cleobury Mortimer ... 23 SO67
Cleobury North ... 23 SO68
Clevedon ... 14 ST47
Cleveleys ... 34 SD34
Cley next the Sea ... 27 TG04
Cliffe ... 12 TQ77
Clifton ... 34 SD43
Cliftonville ... 13 TR37
Climping ... 11 SU90
Clitheroe ... 35 SD74
Clophill ... 25 TL03
Cloughton ... 41 TA09
Clova ... 57 NO37
Clovelly ... 6 SS32
Clowne ... 32 SK47
Clun ... 23 SO38
Clydebank ... 47 NS47
Clynder ... 51 NS28
Clynnog-fawr ... 28 SH44
Clyro ... 22 SO24
Clyst Honiton ... 8 SX99
Coalville ... 31 SK41
Coatbridge ... 47 NS76
Cobham ... 17 TQ16
Cobridge ... 30 SJ84
Cockburnspath ... 49 NT77
Cockenzie and Port Seton ... 48 NT47
Cockermouth ... 43 NY13

Codicote ... 17 TL21
Codnor ... 31 SK44
Codsall ... 23 SJ80
Coggeshall ... 19 TL82
Colby ... 38 SC27
Colchester ... 19 TL92
Coldingham ... 49 NT96
Coleford ... 15 SO51
Colerne ... 15 ST87
Coleshill ... 24 SP28
Colinton ... 48 NT26
Colintraive ... 51 NS07
Collieston ... 63 NK02
Collin ... 43 NY07
Collingham ... 36 SE34
Coln St Aldwyns ... 15 SP10
Colne ... 35 SD83
Colsterworth ... 32 SK92
Coltishall ... 27 TG21
Colvend ... 43 NX85
Colwyn Bay ... 29 SH87
Colyton ... 8 SY29
Combe Martin ... 6 SS54
Combeinteignhead ... 8 SX97
Comrie ... 52 NN72
Congleton ... 30 SJ86
Congresbury ... 14 ST46
Coningsby ... 33 TF25
Conington ... 25 TL18
Conisbrough ... 36 SK59
Coniston ... 38 SD39
Connah's Quay ... 29 SJ26
Connel ... 54 NM93
Conon Bridge ... 60 NH55
Consett ... 45 NZ15
Constantine Bay ... 4 SW87
Contin ... 60 NH45
Conwy ... 29 SH77
Cooden ... 12 TQ70
Cookham ... 16 SU88
Copplestone ... 7 SS70
Copthorne ... 12 TQ33
Corbiere ... 9 JS00
Corbridge ... 45 NY96
Corby ... 25 SP88
Corby Glen ... 32 TF02
Corfe Castle ... 9 SY98
Corgarff ... 57 NJ20
Corhampton ... 10 SU62
Cornhill-on-Tweed ... 49 NT83
Cornwood ... 5 SX65
Corpach ... 55 NN07
Corran ... 59 NG80
Corrie ... 46 NS04
Corris ... 28 SH70
Corse Lawn ... 23 SO83
Corsham ... 15 ST87
Corstorphine ... 48 NT17
Corwen ... 29 SJ04
Coryton ... 12 TQ78
Cosham ... 11 SU60
Coshieville ... 52 NN74
Cottenham ... 18 TL46
Cottered ... 18 TL32
Cottesmore ... 32 SK91
Coulport ... 51 NS28
Coulsdon ... 12 TQ25
Coundon ... 45 NZ22
Countesthorpe ... 25 SP59
Coupar Angus ... 53 NO23
Cove ... 64 NG89
Coventry ... 24 SP37
Coverack ... 4 SW71
Cowbridge ... 14 SS97
Cowdenbeath ... 53 NT19
Cowes ... 10 SZ49
Cowfold ... 11 TQ22
Cowley ... 17 TQ08
Cowley ... 16 SP50
Coxhoe ... 45 NZ33
Coxwold ... 40 SE57
Coylton ... 47 NS41
Coylumbridge ... 56 NH91
Crackington Haven ... 6 SX19
Cradley ... 24 SO98
Cragg Vale ... 35 SE02
Craigellachie ... 61 NJ24
Craighouse ... 50 NR56
Craignure ... 54 NM73
Craigrothie ... 53 NO31
Crail ... 53 NO60
Cramlington ... 45 NZ27
Cramond ... 48 NT17
Cranborne ... 10 SU01
Cranbrook ... 12 TQ73
Cranfield ... 25 SP94
Cranleigh ... 11 TQ03

Crantock ... 4 SW76
Cranwell ... 33 TF04
Crathorne ... 40 NZ40
Craven Arms ... 23 SO48
Crawford ... 48 NS92
Crawfordjohn ... 47 NS82
Crawley ... 12 TQ23
Creag Ghoraidh ... 64 NF74
Creagorry ... 64 NF74
Crediton ... 7 SS80
Creetown ... 42 NX45
Cregneash ... 38 SC16
Cressage ... 23 SJ50
Crewe ... 30 SJ75
Crewkerne ... 9 ST40
Crianlarich ... 55 NN32
Criccieth ... 28 SH43
Crick ... 25 SP57
Crickhowell ... 22 SO21
Cricklade ... 15 SU09
Crieff ... 52 NN82
Crinan ... 51 NR79
Croachy ... 60 NH62
Crockernwell ... 8 SX79
Crocketford ... 43 NX87
Cromarty ... 61 NH76
Cromdale ... 61 NJ02
Cromer ... 27 TG24
Cronton ... 34 SJ48
Crook ... 45 NZ13
Crooklands ... 39 SD58
Crosby ... 38 SC37
Crosby ... 34 SJ39
Cross Hands ... 21 SN51
Cross in Hand ... 12 TQ52
Crossmichael ... 43 NX76
Crossway Green ... 23 SO86
Crosthwaite ... 39 SD49
Croston ... 34 SD41
Crowborough ... 12 TQ53
Crowfield ... 19 TM15
Crowland ... 33 TF21
Crowlas ... 4 SW53
Crowle ... 36 SE71
Crowthorne ... 16 SU86
Croy ... 61 NH74
Croyde ... 6 SS43
Croydon ... 17 TQ36
Cruden Bay ... 63 NK03
Crudgington ... 30 SJ61
Crudwell ... 15 ST99
Crugybar ... 21 SN63
Crumlin ... 14 ST29
Cuckfield ... 12 TQ32
Cuckney ... 32 SK57
Cuddington ... 30 SJ57
Cudworth ... 36 SE30
Cuffley ... 17 TL30
Culcheth ... 34 SJ69
Cullen ... 62 NJ56
Cullercoats ... 45 NZ37
Cullingworth ... 35 SE03
Cullivoe ... 63 HP50
Cullompton ... 7 ST00
Culmstock ... 7 ST11
Culross ... 48 NS98
Cumbernauld ... 47 NS77
Cuminestown ... 62 NJ85
Cummington ... 61 NJ16
Cumnock ... 47 NS52
Cumrew ... 44 NY55
Cupar ... 53 NO31
Cwm-y-glo ... 28 SH56
Cwmbran ... 14 ST29
Cwmystwyth ... 22 SN77
Cymer ... 21 SS89
Cynwyl Elfed ... 21 SN32

Dagenham ... 18 TQ58
Dailly ... 42 NS20
Dalbeattie ... 43 NX86
Dale ... 20 SM80
Dalgety Bay ... 48 NT18
Dalkeith ... 48 NT36
Dallas ... 61 NJ15
Dalmally ... 55 NN12
Dalmellington ... 47 NS40
Dalry ... 47 NS24
Dalrymple ... 47 NS31
Dalston ... 44 NY35

Dalton	43	NY17
Dalwhinnie	56	NN68
Daresbury	30	SJ58
Darlaston	24	SO99
Darley Dale	31	SK26
Darlington	40	NZ21
Darrington	36	SE42
Dartford	12	TQ57
Dartmouth	8	SX85
Darton	35	SE31
Darvel	47	NS53
Darwen	34	SD62
Datchet	17	SU97
Davenham	30	SJ67
Daventry	25	SP56
Daviot	60	NH73
Dawley	30	SJ60
Dawlish	8	SX97
Deal	13	TR35
Deanston	52	NN70
Debenham	19	TM16
Deddington	24	SP43
Dedham	19	TM03
Deeping St. James	33	TF10
Deeping St. Nicholas	33	TF21
Deganwy	29	SH77
Delabole	5	SX08
Delph	35	SD90
Denbigh	29	SJ06
Denby Dale	35	SE20
Denham	17	TQ08
Denholm	48	NT51
Denholme	35	SE03
Dennington	19	TM26
Denny	52	NS88
Denshaw	35	SD91
Dent	39	SD78
Denton	35	SJ99
Derby	31	SK33
Derbyhaven	38	SC26
Dervaig	54	NM45
Desborough	25	SP88
Desford	24	SK40
Devil's Bridge	22	SN77
Devizes	15	SU06
Dewsbury	35	SE22
Dibden Purlieu	10	SU40
Didcot	16	SU59
Dinas-Mawddwy	29	SH81
Dingwall	60	NH55
Dinnet	57	NO49
Dinnington	32	SK58
Dippen	46	NR73
Dirleton	48	NT58
Diseworth	31	SK42
Disley	31	SJ98
Diss	27	TM18
Ditchling	12	TQ31
Ditton Priors	23	SO68
Dobwalls	5	SX26
Docking	26	TF73
Doddington	26	TL49
Doddington	13	TQ95
Doddington	49	NT93
Dodworth	35	SE30
Dolfor	22	SO18
Dolgellau	28	SH71
Dollar	52	NS99
Dolwyddelan	28	SH75
Doncaster	36	SE50
Donington	33	TF23
Dorchester	9	SY69
Dorchester	16	SU59
Dores	60	NH53
Dorking	11	TQ14
Dormington	23	SO54
Dornie	59	NG82
Dornoch	61	NH78
Dorridge	24	SP17
Douglas	38	SC37
Douglas	47	NS83
Dounby	67	HY22
Doune	52	NN70
Dover	13	TR34
Dovercourt	19	TM23
Down Thomas	5	SX55
Downderry	5	SX35
Downton	10	SU12
Draycott	31	SK43
Driffield	41	TA05
Drimnin	54	NM55
Droitwich	23	SO86
Dronfield	31	SK37
Droxford	10	SU61
Drumbeg	65	NC13
Drumclog	47	NS63
Drummore	42	NX13

Drumnadrochit	60	NH53
Drybrook	23	SO61
Drymen	52	NS48
Duddington	25	SK90
Dudley	24	SO99
Duffield	31	SK34
Dufftown	61	NJ34
Duirinish	59	NG73
Dulnain Bridge	61	NH92
Dulverton	7	SS92
Dumbarton	51	NS37
Dumfries	43	NX97
Dunbar	49	NT67
Dunbeath	67	ND12
Dunblane	52	NN70
Dunchurch	24	SP47
Dundee	53	NO43
Dundonnell	59	NH08
Dunfermline	52	NT08
Dunkeld	52	NO04
Dunkirk	13	TR05
Dunnet	67	ND27
Dunning	52	NO01
Dunoon	51	NS17
Dunragit	42	NX15
Duns	49	NT75
Dunscore	43	NX88
Dunsfold	11	TQ03
Dunsop Bridge	34	SD64
Dunstable	17	TL02
Dunster	7	SS94
Duntocher	47	NS47
Duntulm	58	NG47
Dunvegan	58	NG24
Dunwich	27	TM47
Durham	45	NZ24
Durness	65	NC46
Duror	55	NM95
Dursley	15	ST79
Duxford	18	TL44
Dyce	57	NJ81
Dyffryn Ardudwy	28	SH52
Dymchurch	13	TR12
Dysart	53	NT39
Dyserth	29	SJ07

E

Eaglescliffe	40	NZ41
Eaglesfield	44	NY27
Eaglesham	47	NS55
Ealing	17	TQ18
Eamont Bridge	39	NY52
Earby	35	SD94
Earl Shilton	24	SP49
Earls Barton	25	SP86
Earlston	48	NT53
Earsdon	45	NZ37
Easdale	50	NM71
Easington	41	NZ71
Easington	45	NZ44
Easington	37	TA31
Easingwold	40	SE56
East Ayton	41	SE98
East Cowes	10	SZ59
East Dean	12	TV59
East Dereham	27	TF91
East Grinstead	12	TQ33
East Harling	27	TL98
East Horndon	18	TQ68
East Horsley	11	TQ05
East Kilbride	47	NS65
East Linton	48	NT57
East Lulworth	9	SY88
East Portlemouth	8	SX73
East Preston	11	TQ00
East Rudham	26	TF82
East Wittering	11	SZ79
Eastbourne	12	TV69
Eastchurch	13	TQ97
Easter Skeld	63	HU34
Eastfield	41	TA08
Eastham	30	SJ38
Eastleigh	10	SU41
Eastwood	31	SK44
Ebbw Vale	14	SO10
Ebchester	45	NZ15
Ecclefechan	43	NY17
Eccles	49	NT74
Eccles	35	SJ79
Eccleshall	30	SJ82
Echt	57	NJ70

Edderton	60	NH78
Edenbridge	12	TQ44
Edenhall	44	NY53
Edgware	17	TQ19
Edinbane	58	NG35
Edinburgh	48	NT27
Edmonton	17	TQ39
Edmundbyers	45	NZ05
Edwinstowe	32	SK66
Edzell	57	NO66
Egerton	34	SD71
Eggesford	6	SS61
Egglescliffe	40	NZ41
Eggleston	39	NY92
Egham	17	TQ07
Eglingham	49	NU11
Eglwysfach	22	SN69
Eglwyswrw	20	SN13
Egremont	38	NY01
Egton	41	NZ80
Elan Village	22	SN96
Elberton	15	ST68
Elderslie	51	NS46
Elgin	61	NJ26
Elgol	58	NG51
Elie	53	NO40
Elland	35	SE12
Ellesmere	30	SJ33
Ellesmere Port	30	SJ47
Ellingham	27	TM39
Ellon	63	NJ93
Elmstead Market	19	TM02
Elsdon	45	NY99
Elstree	17	TQ19
Elterwater	39	NY30
Eltisley	18	TL25
Elton	25	TL09
Elveden	26	TL88
Elwick	45	NZ43
Ely	26	TL58
Embleton	49	NU22
Embo	66	NH89
Empingham	32	SK90
Emsworth	11	SU70
Endon	31	SJ95
Enfield	17	TQ39
Ennerdale Bridge	38	NY01
Epping	18	TL40
Epsom	17	TQ26
Epworth	36	SE70
Erdington	24	SP19
Eriska	54	NM94
Erith	12	TQ57
Ermington	5	SX65
Errogie	60	NH52
Erskine	47	NS47
Ervie	42	NX06
Erwood	22	SO04
Escrick	36	SE64
Esher	17	TQ16
Eskdale Green	38	NY10
Eskdalemuir	44	NY29
Ettington	24	SP24
Ettrickbridge	44	NT32
Evanton	60	NH66
Evercreech	15	ST63
Evershot	9	ST50
Eversley	16	SU76
Evesham	24	SP04
Ewell	17	TQ26
Ewen	15	SU09
Ewhurst	11	TQ04
Ewloe	29	SJ36
Ewyas Harold	23	SO32
Exbourne	6	SS60
Exebridge	7	SS92
Exeter	8	SX99
Exford	7	SS83
Exmouth	8	SY08
Eye	25	TF20
Eye	27	TM17
Eyemouth	49	NT96
Eynsham	16	SP40

F

Fairbourne	28	SH61
Fairford	15	SP10
Fairlie	46	NS25
Fakenham	26	TF92
Faldingworth	33	TF08
Falfield	15	ST69

Falkirk.................................. 52 NS88
Falkland............................... 53 NO20
Falmouth............................... 4 SW83
Far Sawrey........................... 39 SD39
Fareham............................... 10 SU50
Faringdon............................ 16 SU29
Farnborough........................ 16 SU85
Farnham............................... 11 SU84
Farnham Common................. 17 SU98
Farningham.......................... 12 TQ56
Farnworth............................ 35 SD70
Farrington Gurney................ 15 ST65
Faversham............................ 13 TR06
Fawley................................. 10 SU40
Fazeley............................... 24 SK20
Fearnan............................... 52 NN74
Felbridge............................. 12 TQ33
Felixstowe........................... 19 TM33
Feltham............................... 17 TQ17
Felton................................. 45 NU10
Feltwell.............................. 26 TL79
Fenny Bentley...................... 31 SK14
Fenny Bridges...................... 8 SY19
Fenny Compton..................... 24 SP45
Fenny Drayton..................... 24 SP39
Fenstanton.......................... 18 TL36
Fenwick............................... 47 NS44
Fermain Bay.......................... 4 GN00
Ferndown............................. 10 SU00
Ferness............................... 61 NH94
Ferrybridge.......................... 36 SE42
Ferryhill.............................. 45 NZ23
Fettercairn.......................... 57 NO67
Ffestiniog............................ 28 SH74
Filey................................... 41 TA18
Finchingfield........................ 18 TL63
Finchley............................... 17 TQ29
Findhorn.............................. 61 NJ06
Findochty............................. 62 NJ46
Findon................................. 11 TQ10
Finedon............................... 25 SP97
Finningham........................... 19 TM06
Finstown............................. 67 HY31
Fintry................................. 52 NS68
Fionnphort........................... 54 NM32
Fir Tree.............................. 45 NZ13
Fishbourne........................... 10 SZ59
Fishguard............................. 20 SM93
Fittleworth.......................... 11 TQ01
Five Oaks............................. 9 JS00
Five Oaks............................. 11 TQ02
Fladbury.............................. 24 SO94
Flamborough......................... 41 TA27
Flax Bourton........................ 14 ST56
Fleet.................................. 16 SU85
Fleetwood............................ 34 SD34
Flimby................................ 43 NY03
Flimwell.............................. 12 TQ73
Flint................................... 29 SJ27
Flitwick.............................. 25 TL03
Flockton.............................. 35 SE21
Flodigarry............................ 58 NG47
Flore.................................. 25 SP66
Fochabers............................ 61 NJ35
Folkestone........................... 13 TR23
Fontmell Magna..................... 9 ST81
Fontwell.............................. 11 SU90
Ford................................... 51 NM80
Ford................................... 15 ST87
Forden................................ 23 SJ20
Fordingbridge....................... 10 SU11
Fordoun.............................. 57 NO77
Fordwich............................. 13 TR15
Forest Row........................... 12 TQ43
Forfar................................. 53 NO45
Formby................................ 34 SD30
Forres................................. 61 NJ05
Forsinard............................. 66 NC84
Fort Augustus....................... 60 NH30
Fort William......................... 55 NN17
Forteviot............................. 52 NO01
Forth................................. 47 NS95
Fortingall............................ 52 NN74
Forton................................ 34 SD45
Fortrose.............................. 60 NH75
Fortuneswell......................... 9 SY67
Fossebridge.......................... 15 SP01
Four Marks.......................... 11 SU63
Fowey................................. 5 SX15
Fownhope............................ 23 SO53
Foyers................................ 60 NH42
Fraddon............................... 4 SW95
Fradley............................... 31 SK11
Framlingham......................... 19 TM26
Framwellgate Moor................ 45 NZ24
Fraserburgh......................... 63 NJ96
Freckenham.......................... 26 TL67

Freckleton............................ 34 SD42
Freshwater........................... 10 SZ38
Freswick.............................. 67 ND36
Freuchie.............................. 53 NO20
Fridaythorpe......................... 41 SE85
Frimley................................ 16 SU85
Frinton-on-Sea..................... 19 TM22
Friockheim........................... 53 NO54
Frizington............................ 38 NY01
Frodsham............................. 30 SJ57
Frome................................. 15 ST74
Furnace............................... 51 NN00
Fyfield............................... 16 SU49
Fyvie................................. 62 NJ73

G

Gailey................................ 30 SJ91
Gainsborough........................ 36 SK88
Gairloch.............................. 59 NG87
Gairlochy............................. 55 NN18
Galashiels............................ 48 NT43
Galgate............................... 39 SD45
Galston............................... 47 NS53
Gamlingay............................ 18 TL25
Ganllwyd............................. 28 SH72
Garboldisham........................ 27 TM08
Garelochhead........................ 51 NS29
Garforth.............................. 36 SE43
Gargrave.............................. 35 SD95
Garlieston........................... 42 NX44
Garlogie.............................. 57 NJ70
Garnant............................... 21 SN61
Garrigill.............................. 44 NY74
Garstang.............................. 34 SD44
Garston............................... 30 TL10
Garston............................... 30 SJ48
Garth................................. 22 SN94
Garthmyl.............................. 22 SO19
Garve................................. 60 NH36
Gatehouse of Fleet................. 43 NX55
Gateshead............................ 45 NZ26
Gaydon............................... 24 SP35
Gedney Drove End.................. 33 TF42
Gerrards Cross...................... 17 TQ08
Giffnock.............................. 47 NS55
Gifford............................... 48 NT56
Gillan................................. 4 SW72
Gillingham............................ 15 ST82
Gillingham............................ 12 TQ76
Gilmerton............................ 48 NT26
Gilmerton............................ 52 NN82
Gilwern............................... 23 SO21
Girvan................................ 42 NX19
Gisburn.............................. 35 SD84
Gittisham............................ 8 SY19
Glamis................................ 53 NO34
Glanton............................... 49 NU01
Glapwell.............................. 32 SK46
Glasbury.............................. 22 SO13
Glasgow............................... 47 NS56
Glastonbury.......................... 14 ST53
Glen Maye............................ 38 SC27
Glenbarr.............................. 46 NR63
Glenborrodale....................... 54 NM66
Glenbrittle House.................. 58 NG42
Glencaple............................ 43 NX96
Glencarse............................ 53 NO12
Glencoe............................... 55 NN15
Gleneagles........................... 52 NN90
Glenelg............................... 59 NG81
Glenfarg.............................. 53 NO11
Glenfinnan........................... 54 NM98
Glenkindie........................... 57 NJ41
Glenluce.............................. 42 NX15
Glenridding.......................... 39 NY31
Glenrothes........................... 53 NO20
Glinton............................... 33 TF10
Glossop............................... 35 SK09
Gloucester........................... 23 SO81
Glyn Ceiriog......................... 29 SJ23
Glyn-Neath........................... 21 SN80
Glyncorrwg........................... 21 SS89
Goathland............................ 41 NZ80
Gobowen.............................. 29 SJ33
Godalming............................ 11 SU94
Godmanchester...................... 25 TL27
Godshill.............................. 10 SZ58
Godstone............................. 12 TQ35
Golant................................. 5 SX15
Golspie.............................. 66 NC80
Gomersal............................. 35 SE22

Goodrich.............................. 23 SO51
Goodwick............................. 20 SM93
Goole................................. 36 SE72
Gordon................................ 49 NT64
Gorey................................. 9 JS00
Goring................................ 16 SU68
Goring-by-Sea....................... 11 TQ10
Gorleston on Sea.................. 27 TG50
Gorseinon............................ 21 SS59
Gosberton............................ 33 TF23
Gosforth.............................. 38 NY00
Gosforth.............................. 45 NZ26
Gosport............................... 10 SZ69
Goudhurst............................ 12 TQ73
Gowerton............................. 21 SS59
Grain................................. 13 TQ87
Gramsdal.............................. 64 NF85
Grand Chemins........................ 9 JS00
Grandes Rocques..................... 9 GN00
Grandtully............................ 52 NN95
Grange................................ 38 NY21
Grange-over-Sands.................. 39 SD47
Grangemouth......................... 52 NS98
Grangetown........................... 40 NZ52
Grantham.............................. 32 SK93
Grantown-on-Spey................... 61 NJ02
Grantshouse.......................... 49 NT86
Grasmere.............................. 39 NY30
Grassington.......................... 40 SE06
Graveley.............................. 18 TL22
Gravesend............................ 12 TQ67
Grays................................. 12 TQ67
Great Asby........................... 39 NY61
Great Ayton.......................... 40 NZ51
Great Badminton.................... 15 ST88
Great Barr............................ 24 SP09
Great Bircham....................... 26 TF73
Great Blakenham.................... 19 TM15
Great Bookham....................... 17 TQ15
Great Chesterford.................. 18 TL54
Great Dunmow........................ 18 TL62
Great Gidding....................... 25 TL18
Great Glen........................... 25 SP69
Great Haywood....................... 31 SJ92
Great Kimble......................... 16 SP80
Great Langdale...................... 38 NY20
Great Leighs......................... 18 TL71
Great Malvern........................ 23 SO74
Great Milton......................... 16 SP60
Great Missenden..................... 16 SP80
Great Ponton......................... 32 SK93
Great Shelford....................... 18 TL45
Great Staughton..................... 25 TL16
Great Torrington..................... 6 SS41
Great Wakering...................... 19 TQ98
Great Weldon......................... 25 SP98
Great Witley......................... 23 SO76
Great Yarmouth...................... 27 TG50
Great Yeldham........................ 18 TL73
Greatstone-on-Sea.................. 13 TR02
Green Hammerton.................... 40 SE45
Greenfield............................ 29 SJ17
Greenford............................ 17 TQ18
Greenhead............................ 44 NY66
Greenlaw.............................. 49 NT74
Greenloaning......................... 52 NN80
Greenock.............................. 51 NS27
Greetland............................ 35 SE02
Greta Bridge......................... 40 NZ01
Gretna................................ 44 NY36
Gretna Green......................... 44 NY36
Greystoke............................ 44 NY43
Grimsargh............................ 34 SD53
Grimsby............................... 37 TA21
Grimston.............................. 26 TF72
Grindleford........................... 31 SK27
Gringley on the Hill................ 36 SK79
Grizedale............................ 39 SD39
Groby................................. 32 SK50
Gronant............................... 29 SJ08
Grosmont............................. 41 NZ80
Grouville.............................. 9 JS00
Guardbridge.......................... 53 NO41
Guildford............................. 11 SU94
Guilsborough......................... 25 SP67
Guisborough.......................... 40 NZ61
Guiseley.............................. 35 SE14
Guist................................. 27 TG02
Gullane............................... 48 NT48
Gulworthy.............................. 5 SX47
Gunnislake............................ 5 SX47
Gunthorpe............................ 32 SK64
Gurnard.............................. 10 SZ49
Guthrie............................... 53 NO55
Gutcher............................... 63 HU59
Guyhirn............................... 26 TF40
Gwbert on Sea....................... 20 SN15

Gweek.................................. 4 SW72
Gwernymynydd.................... 29 SJ26
Gwithian.............................. 4 SW54

Hackness............................ 41 SE99
Haddenham......................... 16 SP70
Haddenham......................... 26 TL47
Haddington......................... 48 NT57
Haddiscoe........................... 27 TM49
Hadleigh............................. 18 TQ88
Hadleigh............................. 19 TM04
Hadley Wood...................... 17 TQ29
Hailsham............................ 12 TQ50
Hainault.............................. 18 TQ49
Halesowen.......................... 24 SO98
Halesworth......................... 27 TM37
Halifax................................ 35 SE02
Halkirk............................... 67 ND15
Halkyn................................ 29 SJ27
Halland............................... 12 TQ41
Hallworthy.......................... 5 SX18
Halstead............................. 18 TL83
Halwell............................... 8 SX75
Hamble................................ 10 SU40
Hambleton.......................... 36 SE53
Hamilton............................. 47 NS75
Hamnavoe........................... 63 HU33
Hampson Green.................. 34 SD45
Hampstead Norrey's............ 16 SU57
Hampsthwaite..................... 40 SE25
Hampton............................ 17 TQ16
Hampton in Arden............... 24 SP28
Hamstreet........................... 13 TR03
Hanchurch.......................... 30 SJ84
Handcross........................... 12 TQ22
Handforth............................ 30 SJ88
Handley............................... 30 SJ45
Handsacre........................... 31 SK01
Handsworth......................... 24 SP08
Hanford............................... 30 SJ84
Hanley................................. 30 SJ84
Hanslope............................. 25 SP84
Happisburgh........................ 27 TG33
Harborne............................ 24 SP08
Hare Street......................... 18 TL32
Harewood............................ 35 SE34
Harlech............................... 28 SH53
Harleston............................ 27 TM28
Harlosh............................... 58 NG24
Harlow................................ 18 TL41
Harlyn Bay........................... 4 SW87
Harold Wood....................... 18 TQ59
Haroldswick......................... 63 HP61
Harome................................ 40 SE68
Harpenden.......................... 17 TL11
Harrogate............................ 35 SE35
Harrold............................... 25 SP95
Harrow................................ 17 TQ18
Harrow Weald..................... 17 TQ19
Hartfield.............................. 12 TQ43
Hartford.............................. 30 SJ67
Harthill............................... 47 NS96
Hartington.......................... 31 SK16
Hartland.............................. 6 SS22
Hartlebury.......................... 23 SO87
Hartlepool.......................... 45 NZ53
Hartley Wintney................. 16 SU75
Harvington......................... 24 SP04
Harwich.............................. 19 TM23
Haslemere.......................... 11 SU93
Haslingden......................... 35 SD72
Hassocks............................ 12 TQ31
Hastings.............................. 12 TQ80
Hatch Beauchamp............... 8 ST32
Hatfield.............................. 17 TL20
Hatfield.............................. 36 SE60
Hatfield Heath.................... 18 TL51
Hatherleigh......................... 6 SS50
Hathern.............................. 32 SK52
Hathersage......................... 31 SK28
Hatton................................ 63 NK03
Haughton le Skerne............ 40 NZ31
Hautes Croix....................... 9 JS00
Havant................................ 11 SU70
Havenstreet........................ 10 SZ59
Haverfordwest.................... 20 SM91
Haverhill............................. 18 TL64
Hawarden........................... 29 SJ36
Hawes................................ 39 SD88
Hawick............................... 48 NT51

Hawkchurch........................ 9 ST30
Hawkhurst.......................... 12 TQ73
Hawkinge............................ 13 TR23
Hawkshead......................... 39 SD39
Hawnby.............................. 40 SE58
Haworth.............................. 35 SE03
Haxby................................. 40 SE65
Hay-on-Wye....................... 23 SO24
Haydock.............................. 34 SJ59
Haydon Bridge................... 44 NY86
Hayes................................. 17 TQ08
Hayle.................................. 4 SW53
Haytor Vale........................ 8 SX77
Haywards Heath................. 12 TQ32
Hazel Grove........................ 30 SJ98
Heacham............................. 26 TF63
Headcorn............................ 13 TQ84
Headingley.......................... 35 SE23
Heanor................................ 31 SK44
Heathfield........................... 12 TQ52
Hebburn.............................. 45 NZ36
Hebden Bridge................... 35 SD92
Heckfield............................ 16 SU76
Heckington......................... 33 TF14
Hedge End.......................... 10 SU41
Hednesford......................... 31 SJ91
Hedon................................. 37 TA12
Heighington........................ 40 NZ22
Helensburgh....................... 51 NS28
Hellidon.............................. 24 SP55
Hellifield............................. 39 SD85
Helmingham........................ 19 TM15
Helmsdale........................... 67 ND01
Helmsley............................. 40 SE68
Helpringham....................... 33 TF14
Helsby................................ 30 SJ47
Helston............................... 4 SW62
Hemel Hempstead.............. 17 TL00
Hemingford Abbots............ 26 TL27
Hempnall............................ 27 TM29
Hempstead.......................... 23 SO81
Hemsby............................... 27 TG41
Hemsworth.......................... 36 SE41
Hemyock............................. 7 ST11
Henfield.............................. 11 TQ21
Henley-in-Arden................. 24 SP16
Henley-on-Thames.............. 16 SU78
Henllan............................... 29 SJ06
Henlow............................... 25 TL13
Henstridge.......................... 15 ST71
Hereford............................. 23 SO53
Hermitage........................... 16 SU57
Herne Bay.......................... 13 TR16
Herstmonceux.................... 12 TQ61
Hertford.............................. 17 TL31
Hesketh Bank..................... 34 SD42
Hesleden............................ 45 NZ43
Hessle................................. 37 TA02
Heswall............................... 29 SJ28
Hethersett.......................... 27 TG10
Hetton-le-Hole.................... 45 NZ34
Heversham.......................... 39 SD48
Hexham............................... 45 NY96
Hexworthy........................... 5 SX67
Heysham............................. 39 SD46
Heytesbury......................... 15 ST94
Heywood............................. 35 SD81
Hickstead........................... 12 TQ22
High Bentham..................... 39 SD66
High Ercall......................... 30 SJ51
High Halden........................ 13 TQ83
High Hesket........................ 44 NY44
High Wycombe.................... 16 SU89
Higham Ferrers.................. 25 SP96
Highampton........................ 6 SS40
Highbridge.......................... 14 ST34
Highcliffe............................ 10 SZ29
Higher Burwardsley............ 30 SJ55
Higher Penwortham............ 34 SD52
Higher Town....................... 4 SV91
Highley............................... 23 SO78
Highworth........................... 15 SU29
Hildenborough.................... 12 TQ54
Hill of Fearn....................... 61 NH87
Hillingdon........................... 17 TQ08
Hillington............................ 26 TF72
Hillswick............................. 63 HU27
Hilton................................. 31 SK23
Himley................................ 23 SO89
Hinckley.............................. 24 SP49
Hindhead............................ 11 SU83
Hindley............................... 34 SD60
Hindon................................ 15 ST93
Hingham............................. 27 TG00
Hintlesham.......................... 19 TM04
Hinton Charterhouse.......... 15 ST75

Hirwaun.............................. 14 SN90
Hitchin............................... 25 TL12
Hockley Heath.................... 24 SP17
Hockliffe............................. 25 SP92
Hoddesdon......................... 18 TL30
Hoddlesden......................... 34 SD72
Hodnet................................ 30 SJ62
Holbeach............................. 33 TF32
Holbeton............................. 5 SX65
Holford............................... 14 ST14
Holkham............................. 26 TF84
Holland-on-Sea................... 19 TM11
Hollingbourne..................... 13 TQ85
Hollingworth....................... 35 SK09
Hollywood........................... 24 SP07
Holmbury St. Mary............ 11 TQ14
Holme Chapel..................... 35 SD82
Holme upon Spalding Moor 36 SE83
Holmes Chapel................... 30 SJ76
Holmfirth............................ 35 SE10
Holmrook............................ 38 SD09
Holne................................. 8 SX76
Holsworthy.......................... 6 SS30
Holt................................... 30 SJ45
Holt................................... 27 TG03
Holy Island......................... 49 NU14
Holyhead............................ 28 SH28
Holywell.............................. 29 SJ17
Holywell Green.................... 35 SE01
Homersfield........................ 27 TM28
Honiley............................... 24 SP27
Honiton.............................. 8 ST10
Honley................................ 35 SE11
Hoo................................... 12 TQ77
Hook.................................. 16 SU75
Hope.................................. 31 SK18
Hope.................................. 8 SX64
Hope under Dinmore.......... 23 SO55
Hopeman............................ 61 NJ16
Hopton on Sea.................... 27 TM59
Horley................................ 12 TQ24
Hornby............................... 39 SD56
Horncastle.......................... 33 TF26
Hornchurch......................... 18 TQ58
Horndean............................ 11 SU71
Horning.............................. 27 TG31
Hornsea.............................. 37 TA14
Horrabridge........................ 5 SX56
Horsey............................... 27 TG42
Horsforth............................ 35 SE23
Horsham............................. 11 TQ13
Horsington.......................... 15 ST72
Horton............................... 8 ST31
Horton in Ribblesdale......... 39 SD87
Horton-cum-Studley............ 16 SP51
Horwich.............................. 34 SD61
Hothfield............................ 13 TQ94
Hough Green...................... 30 SJ48
Houghton le Spring............ 45 NZ34
Houghton on the Hill.......... 25 SK60
Hounslow............................ 17 TQ17
Houton............................... 67 HY30
Hove.................................. 12 TQ20
Hovingham.......................... 40 SE67
How Caple.......................... 23 SO63
Howden.............................. 36 SE72
Howtown............................ 39 NY41
Howwood............................ 47 NS36
Hoylake.............................. 34 SJ28
Hoyland Nether.................. 36 SE30
Hucknall............................. 32 SK54
Huddersfield....................... 35 SE11
Hugh Town......................... 4 SV91
Hull................................... 37 TA02
Humberston......................... 37 TA30
Humbie............................... 48 NT46
Hungerford......................... 16 SU36
Hunmanby.......................... 41 TA07
Hunstanton......................... 26 TF64
Hunstrete............................ 15 ST66
Hunters Quay..................... 51 NS17
Huntingdon......................... 25 TL27
Huntley.............................. 23 SO71
Huntly................................ 62 NJ53
Hurley................................ 16 SU88
Hurst................................. 16 SU77
Hurst................................. 12 TQ72
Hurst Green........................ 12 TQ72
Hurst Green........................ 34 SD63
Hurstbourne Priors............. 10 SU44
Hurstbourne Tarrant........... 16 SU35
Husbands Bosworth............ 25 SP68
Husborne Crawley............... 25 SP93
Hutton................................ 34 SD42
Hutton................................ 8 SE79
Hutton-le-Hole................... 41 SE79
Huyton............................... 34 SJ49
Hyde.................................. 35 SJ99
Hynish............................... 50 NL93

Hythe...................................... 10 SU40
Hythe...................................... 13 TR13

I

Ibstock................................. 31 SK40
Ideford................................... 8 SX87
Ilchester............................. 14 ST52
Ilford................................. 18 TQ48
Ilfracombe............................. 6 SS54
Ilkeston............................. 31 SK44
Ilkley............................. 35 SE14
Illingworth............................. 35 SE02
Ilminster............................. 9 ST31
Ilsington............................. 8 SX77
Immingham............................. 37 TA11
Immingham Dock............................. 37 TA11
Ince Blundell............................. 34 SD30
Inchnadamph............................. 65 NC22
Ingatestone............................. 18 TQ69
Ingleton............................. 39 SD67
Ingoldisthorpe............................. 26 TF63
Ingoldmells............................. 33 TF56
Inkberrow............................. 24 SP05
Innellan............................. 51 NS17
Innerleithen............................. 48 NT33
Insch............................. 62 NJ62
Insh............................. 56 NH80
Instow............................. 6 SS43
Inverallochy............................. 63 NK06
Inveraray............................. 51 NN00
Inverey............................. 56 NO08
Inverfarigaig............................. 60 NH52
Invergarry............................. 55 NH30
Invergordon............................. 60 NH76
Inverkeilor............................. 53 NO64
Inverkeithing............................. 48 NT18
Inverkip............................. 51 NS27
Inverkirkaig............................. 65 NC01
Invermoriston............................. 60 NH41
Inverness............................. 60 NH64
Invershin............................. 66 NH59
Inversnaid Hotel............................. 51 NN30
Inverurie............................. 57 NJ72
Ipplepen............................. 8 SX86
Ipswich............................. 19 TM14
Irby............................. 29 SJ28
Irlam............................. 34 SJ79
Ironbridge............................. 23 SJ60
Irthlingborough............................. 25 SP97
Irvine............................. 47 NS33
Isbister............................. 63 HU39
Isle of Whithorn............................. 42 NX43
Islet Village............................. 9 GN00
Iver............................. 17 TQ08
Iver Heath............................. 17 TQ08
Ivinghoe............................. 17 SP91
Ivybridge............................. 5 SX65
Iwade............................. 13 TQ96
Ixworth............................. 27 TL97

J

Jedburgh............................. 49 NT62
Jerbourg............................. 48 GN00
John O'Groats............................. 67 ND37
Johnshaven............................. 57 NO76
Johnston............................. 20 SM91
Johnstone............................. 51 NS46
Jurby............................. 38 SC39

K

Kames............................. 51 NR97
Kegworth............................. 32 SK42
Keighley............................. 35 SE04
Keiss............................. 67 ND36
Keith............................. 62 NJ45
Keld............................. 39 NY80
Kelling............................. 27 TG04
Kelso............................. 49 NT73
Kelvedon............................. 19 TL81

Kemble............................. 15 ST99
Kemnay............................. 57 NJ71
Kempston............................. 25 TL04
Kempston Hardwick............................. 25 TL04
Kendal............................. 39 SD59
Kenilworth............................. 24 SP27
Kenmore............................. 52 NN74
Kennacraig............................. 51 NR86
Kennet............................. 52 NS99
Kennethmont............................. 62 NJ52
Kennford............................. 8 SX98
Kenninghall............................. 27 TM08
Kensworth............................. 25 TL01
Kentallen............................. 55 NN05
Kentra............................. 54 NM66
Kerne Bridge............................. 23 SO51
Kessingland............................. 27 TM58
Keswick............................. 38 NY22
Kettering............................. 25 SP87
Kettletoft............................. 67 HY63
Kettlewell............................. 39 SD97
Keynsham............................. 15 ST66
Kibworth Harcourt............................. 25 SP69
Kidderminster............................. 23 SO87
Kidlington............................. 16 SP41
Kidsgrove............................. 30 SJ85
Kidwelly............................. 21 SN40
Kielder............................. 44 NY69
Kilberry............................. 50 NR76
Kilbirnie............................. 47 NS35
Kilburn............................. 40 SE57
Kilchattan............................. 46 NS15
Kilchrenan............................. 51 NN02
Kilcreggan............................. 51 NS28
Kildrummy............................. 57 NJ41
Kilfinan............................. 51 NR97
Kilkhampton............................. 6 SS21
Killearn............................. 52 NS58
Killiechronan............................. 54 NM54
Killiecrankie............................. 56 NN96
Killin............................. 52 NN53
Kilmacolm............................. 51 NS36
Kilmaluag............................. 58 NG47
Kilmarnock............................. 47 NS43
Kilmartin............................. 51 NR89
Kilmaurs............................. 47 NS44
Kilmelford............................. 51 NM81
Kilmore............................. 58 NG60
Kilmory............................. 50 NR77
Kilninver............................. 51 NM82
Kilnsea............................. 37 TA41
Kilsby............................. 24 SP57
Kilsyth............................. 52 NS77
Kilve............................. 7 ST14
Kilwinning............................. 47 NS34
Kimberley............................. 27 TG00
Kimbolton............................. 25 TL16
Kinbrace............................. 66 NC83
Kinbuck............................. 52 NN70
Kincardine............................. 52 NS98
Kincardine O'Neil............................. 57 NO59
Kinclaven............................. 53 NO13
Kincraig............................. 56 NH80
Kineton............................. 24 SP35
King's Bromley............................. 31 SK11
King's Lynn............................. 26 TF62
King's Mills............................. 26 GN00
Kingham............................. 16 SP22
Kinghorn............................. 48 NT28
Kings Langley............................. 17 TL00
Kingsbarns............................. 53 NO51
Kingsbridge............................. 8 SX74
Kingsbury............................. 24 SP29
Kingsclere............................. 16 SU55
Kingsdown............................. 13 TR34
Kingseat............................. 52 NT19
Kingsfold............................. 11 TQ13
Kingskerswell............................. 8 SX86
Kingsley............................. 30 SJ57
Kingstanding............................. 24 SP09
Kingsteignton............................. 8 SX87
Kingston Bagpuize............................. 16 SU49
Kingston on Spey............................. 61 NJ36
Kingston upon Thames............................. 17 TQ16
Kingswear............................. 8 SX85
Kingswinford............................. 23 SO88
Kington............................. 23 SO25
Kingussie............................. 56 NH70
Kinloch Hourn............................. 59 NG90
Kinloch Rannoch............................. 52 NN65
Kinlochard............................. 52 NN40
Kinlochbervie............................. 65 NC25
Kinlocheil............................. 55 NM97
Kinlochewe............................. 59 NH06
Kinlochleven............................. 55 NN16
Kinlochmoidart............................. 54 NM77
Kinloss............................. 61 NJ06

Kinnesswood............................. 53 NO10
Kinross............................. 53 NO10
Kintore............................. 57 NJ71
Kippen............................. 52 NS69
Kirby Misperton............................. 41 SE77
Kirby Muxloe............................. 31 SK50
Kirk Langley............................. 31 SK23
Kirk Michael............................. 38 SC39
Kirkbean............................. 43 NX95
Kirkbride............................. 44 NY25
Kirkburton............................. 35 SE11
Kirkby............................. 34 SJ49
Kirkby Fleetham............................. 40 SE29
Kirkby in Ashfield............................. 32 SK45
Kirkby Lonsdale............................. 39 SD67
Kirkby Malzeard............................. 40 SE27
Kirkby Stephen............................. 39 NY70
Kirkby-in-Furness............................. 38 SD28
Kirkbymoorside............................. 41 SE68
Kirkcaldy............................. 53 NT29
Kirkcolm............................. 42 NX06
Kirkcowan............................. 42 NX36
Kirkcudbright............................. 43 NX65
Kirkham............................. 34 SD43
Kirkhill............................. 60 NH54
Kirkintilloch............................. 47 NS67
Kirkmichael............................. 47 NS30
Kirkmichael............................. 56 NO05
Kirknewton............................. 48 NT16
Kirknewton............................. 49 NT93
Kirkpatrick-Fleming............................. 44 NY27
Kirkwall............................. 67 HY41
Kirkwhelpington............................. 45 NY98
Kirriemuir............................. 53 NO35
Kirton in Lindsey............................. 36 SK99
Knaresborough............................. 40 SE35
Knebworth............................. 17 TL22
Knighton............................. 23 SO27
Knightwick............................. 23 SO75
Knockan............................. 65 NC21
Knockin............................. 29 SJ32
Knottingley............................. 36 SE52
Knowle............................. 24 SP17
Knowsley............................. 34 SJ49
Knutsford............................. 30 SJ77
Kyle of Lochalsh............................. 59 NG72
Kyleakin............................. 59 NG72
Kylerhea............................. 59 NG72
Kylestrome............................. 65 NC23

L

L'Eree............................. 65 GN00
L'Etacq............................. 9 JS00
Laceby............................. 37 TA20
Ladybank............................. 53 NO30
Lagg............................. 46 NR92
Laggan............................. 56 NN69
Laide............................. 64 NG99
Lairg............................. 66 NC50
Lamberhurst............................. 12 TQ63
Lambourn............................. 16 SU37
Lamlash............................. 46 NS03
Lamorna............................. 4 SW42
Lampeter............................. 21 SN54
Lamport............................. 25 SP77
Lanark............................. 47 NS84
Lancaster............................. 39 SD46
Lanchester............................. 45 NZ14
Lancing............................. 11 TQ10
Landcross............................. 6 SS42
Lands End............................. 4 SW32
Langar............................. 32 SK73
Langbank............................. 51 NS37
Langholm............................. 44 NY38
Langland............................. 21 SS68
Langley Park............................. 45 NZ24
Langport............................. 14 ST42
Langsett............................. 35 SE20
Langstone............................. 14 ST38
Langthwaite............................. 40 NZ00
Langtoft............................. 41 TA06
Langtoft............................. 33 TF11
Langwathby............................. 44 NY53
Lanivet............................. 5 SX06
Lanreath............................. 5 SX15
Lapford............................. 7 SS70
Larbert............................. 52 NS88
Largoward............................. 53 NO40
Largs............................. 46 NS25
Larkfield............................. 12 TQ75
Larkhall............................. 47 NS75

Lasswade 48 NT36
Lastingham 41 SE79
Latchingdon 19 TL80
Latheron 67 ND23
Lauder 48 NT54
Laugharne 20 SN31
Launceston 5 SX38
Laurencekirk 57 NO77
Laurieston 43 NX66
Lavenham 19 TL94
Laverstoke 10 SU44
Lawers 52 NN63
Laxey 38 SC48
Laxford Bridge 65 NC24
Laxo 63 HU46
Lazonby 44 NY53
Le Bourg 44 GN00
Lea Marston 24 SP29
Leadburn 48 NT25
Leaden Roding 18 TL51
Leadenham 32 SK95
Leadhills 47 NS81
Leamington Spa 24 SP36
Leatherhead 17 TQ15
Lechlade 15 SU29
Leckmelm 65 NH18
Ledbury 23 SO73
Ledmore Junction 65 NC21
Lee 6 SS44
Lee-on-the-Solent 10 SU50
Leeds 35 SE23
Leedstown 4 SW63
Leek 31 SJ95
Leeming Bar 40 SE28
Leicester 25 SK50
Leigh 9 ST60
Leigh 34 SJ69
Leigh 12 TQ54
Leigh-on-Sea 19 TQ88
Leighton Buzzard 16 SP92
Leintwardine 23 SO47
Leiston 19 TM46
Leith 48 NT27
Lelant 4 SW53
Lendalfoot 42 NX19
Lenham 13 TQ85
Lennoxtown 52 NS67
Lenzie 47 NS67
Leominster 23 SO45
Lerwick 63 HU44
Leslie 53 NO20
Leswalt 42 NX06
Letchworth 18 TL23
Letham 53 NO31
Letham 53 NO54
Letterfinlay Lodge Hotel 55 NN29
Letterston 20 SM92
Leuchars 53 NO42
Leven 53 NO30
Leven 37 TA14
Levens 39 SD48
Lewdown 5 SX48
Lewes 12 TQ41
Leyburn 40 SE19
Leyland 34 SD52
Leysdown-on-Sea 13 TR07
Lichfield 31 SK10
Lifton 5 SX38
Lightwater 17 SU96
Lilliesleaf 48 NT52
Limpley Stoke 15 ST76
Lincoln 32 SK97
Lindford 11 SU83
Lingfield 12 TQ34
Linlithgow 48 NS97
Linton 18 TL54
Linwood 51 NS46
Liphook 11 SU83
Liskeard 5 SX26
Liss 11 SU72
Little Berkhamsted 17 TL20
Little Brickhill 25 SP93
Little Chalfont 16 SU99
Little Compton 24 SP23
Little Hulton 34 SD70
Little Langdale 38 NY30
Little Walsingham 27 TF93
Little Weighton 37 SE93
Littleborough 35 SD91
Littlebourne 13 TR25
Littlehampton 11 TQ00
Littleport 26 TL58
Littlestone-on-Sea 13 TR02
Liverpool 34 SJ39
Liversedge 35 SE12
Livingston 48 NT06
Lizard 4 SW71

Llanaelhaearn 28 SH34
Llanarmon Dyffryn Ceiriog 29 SJ13
Llanarth 21 SN45
Llanbedr 28 SH52
Llanbedr-Dyffryn-Clwyd 29 SJ15
Llanberis 28 SH56
Llanbister 22 SO17
Llanbrynmair 22 SH80
Llanddarog 21 SN51
Llanddeiniolen 28 SH56
Llandderfel 29 SH93
Llandegla 29 SJ25
Llandeilo 21 SN62
Llandissilio 20 SN12
Llandogo 14 SO50
Llandovery 21 SN73
Llandrillo 29 SJ03
Llandrindod Wells 22 SO06
Llandudno 29 SH78
Llandudno Junction 29 SH77
Llandybie 21 SN61
Llandysul 21 SN44
Llanelli 21 SN50
Llanerchymedd 28 SH48
Llanfachraeth 28 SH38
Llanfair Caereinion 29 SJ10
Llanfair Dyffryn Clwyd 29 SJ15
Llanfair P G 28 SH57
Llanfair Talhaiarn 29 SH97
Llanfairfechan 28 SH67
Llanfihangel-nant-Melan 22 SO15
Llanfyllin 29 SJ11
Llangadfan 29 SJ01
Llangadog 21 SN72
Llangammarch Wells 22 SN94
Llangefni 28 SH47
Llangennith 21 SS49
Llangernyw 29 SH86
Llangoed 28 SH67
Llangollen 29 SJ24
Llangors 22 SO12
Llangranog 20 SN35
Llangurig 22 SN97
Llangybi 14 ST39
Llangynidr 22 SO11
Llangynog 29 SJ02
Llanharan 14 ST08
Llanidloes 22 SN98
Llanilar 22 SN67
Llanllwni 21 SN44
Llanrhaeadr-ym-Mochnant 29 SJ12
Llanrhidian 21 SS49
Llanrhystud 22 SN56
Llanrwst 29 SH86
Llansamlet 21 SS69
Llansanffraid Glan Conwy ... 29 SH87
Llansannan 29 SH96
Llansantffraid 22 SN56
Llansantffraid-ym-Mechain 29 SJ22
Llansawel 21 SN63
Llansteffan 21 SN31
Llanthony 23 SO22
Llantrisant 14 ST08
Llantwit Major 7 SS96
Llanuwchllyn 29 SH83
Llanvetherine 23 SO31
Llanvihangel Crucorney 23 SO32
Llanwddyn 29 SJ01
Llanwnda 28 SH45
Llanwrda 21 SN73
Llanwrtyd Wells 22 SN84
Llanybydder 21 SN54
Llanymynech 29 SJ22
Llechryd 20 SN24
Llwyngwril 28 SH50
Llynclys 29 SJ22
Llyswen 22 SO13
Loanhead 48 NT26
Loch Baghasdail 64 NF71
Loch nam Madadh 58 NF96
Lochailort 54 NM78
Lochaline 54 NM64
Locharbriggs 43 NX98
Lochawe 55 NN12
Lochboisdale 64 NF71
Lochbuie 54 NM62
Lochcarron 59 NG83
Lochdon 54 NM73
Lochearnhead 52 NN52
Lochgair 51 NR99
Lochgelly 53 NT19
Lochgilphead 51 NR88
Lochgoilhead 51 NN20
Lochinver 65 NC02
Lochmaben 43 NY08
Lochmaddy 64 NF96
Lochranza 46 NR95

Lochwinnoch 47 NS35
Lockerbie 43 NY18
Loddon 27 TM39
Lofthouse 35 SE32
Loftus 41 NZ71
Lolworth 18 TL36
London 17 TQ27
Long Buckby 25 SP66
Long Crendon 16 SP60
Long Eaton 32 SK43
Long Melford 19 TL84
Long Preston 39 SD85
Long Stratton 27 TM19
Long Sutton 33 TF42
Longbridge Deverill 15 ST84
Longdown 8 SX89
Longformacus 49 NT65
Longframlington 45 NU10
Longham 10 SZ09
Longhorsley 45 NZ19
Longhoughton 45 NU21
Longniddry 48 NT47
Longnor 23 SJ40
Longnor 31 SK06
Longridge 34 SD63
Longton 34 SD42
Longton 39 SJ94
Longueville 9 JS00
Longville in the Dale 23 SO59
Looe 5 SX25
Lossiemouth 61 NJ27
Lostwithiel 5 SX15
Loughborough 32 SK51
Loughor 21 SS59
Loughton 18 TQ49
Louth 33 TF38
Low Eggborough 36 SE52
Lowdham 32 SK64
Lower Beeding 11 TQ22
Lower Diabaig 59 NG76
Lower Slaughter 24 SP12
Lowestoft 27 TM59
Loweswater 38 NY12
Lowick 49 NU03
Ludborough 37 TF29
Luddenden 35 SE02
Ludgershall 10 SU25
Ludlow 23 SO57
Ludwell 15 ST92
Lugton 47 NS45
Lugwardine 23 SO54
Lumby 36 SE43
Lumphanan 57 NJ50
Lumsden 57 NJ42
Lunan 53 NO65
Lundin Links 53 NO40
Luss 51 NS39
Luton 17 TL02
Lutterworth 24 SP58
Lybster 67 ND23
Lydd 13 TR02
Lyddington 25 SP89
Lydford 5 SX58
Lydford on Fosse 14 ST53
Lydham 23 SO39
Lydney 15 SO60
Lye 24 SO98
Lyme Regis 9 SY39
Lyminge 13 TR14
Lymington 10 SZ39
Lymm 30 SJ68
Lympsham 14 ST35
Lyndhurst 10 SU30
Lyneham 15 SU07
Lyness 67 ND39
Lynmouth 6 SS74
Lynton 6 SS74
Lytham St. Anne's 34 SD32

Mablethorpe 33 TF58
Macclesfield 30 SJ97
Macduff 62 NJ76
Machrie 46 NR83
Machrihanish 46 NR62
Machynlleth 28 SH70
Madeley 30 SJ74
Maerdy 14 SS99
Maesteg 21 SS89
Maiden Bradley 15 ST83
Maiden Newton 9 SY59

Maidencombe	8	SX96
Maidenhead	16	SU88
Maidstone	12	TQ75
Mainsriddle	43	NX95
Maldon	19	TL80
Malham	39	SD96
Mallaig	54	NM69
Mallwyd	29	SH81
Malmesbury	15	ST98
Malpas	30	SJ44
Maltby	36	SK59
Malton	41	SE77
Manaccan	4	SW72
Manchester	35	SJ89
Manea	26	TL48
Manorbier	20	SS09
Mansfield	32	SK56
Mansfield Woodhouse	32	SK56
Manston	13	TR36
Marazion	4	SW53
March	26	TL49
Marcham	16	SU49
Marchwiel	30	SJ34
Marden	12	TQ74
Mareham le Fen	33	TF26
Maresfield	12	TQ42
Margate	13	TR37
Marian-glas	28	SH58
Market Bosworth	24	SK40
Market Deeping	33	TF11
Market Drayton	30	SJ63
Market Harborough	25	SP78
Market Rasen	37	TF18
Market Weighton	36	SE84
Markfield	32	SK40
Markham Moor	32	SK77
Markinch	53	NO20
Markington	40	SE26
Marks Tey	19	TL92
Markyate	17	TL01
Marlborough	15	SU16
Marldon	8	SX86
Marlow	16	SU88
Marnhull	9	ST71
Marple	35	SJ98
Marsden	35	SE01
Marshfield	15	ST77
Marske-by-the-Sea	40	NZ62
Marston Magna	15	ST52
Marston Moretaine	25	SP94
Marston Trussell	25	SP68
Martinhoe	6	SS64
Martock	9	ST41
Marton	40	NZ51
Mary Tavy	5	SX57
Marykirk	57	NO66
Maryport	43	NY03
Masham	40	SE28
Matlock	31	SK35
Matlock Bath	31	SK25
Mattingley	16	SU75
Mauchline	47	NS42
Maughold	38	SC49
Mawdesley	34	SD41
Mawgan Porth	4	SW86
Mawnan Smith	4	SW72
Maybole	47	NS20
Mayfield	12	TQ52
Mealsgate	43	NY24
Measham	31	SK31
Meigle	53	NO24
Melbourne	31	SK32
Melksham	15	ST96
Melling	39	SD57
Melmerby	44	NY63
Meltham	35	SE11
Melton	36	SE92
Melton Constable	27	TG03
Melton Mowbray	32	SK71
Melvaig	59	NG78
Melvich	66	NC86
Membury	8	ST20
Memsie	63	NJ96
Menai Bridge	28	SH57
Mendham	27	TM28
Mere	30	SJ78
Mere	15	ST83
Meriden	24	SP28
Merstham	11	TQ25
Merthyr Tydfil	14	SO00
Messingham	36	SE80
Metheringham	33	TF06
Methlick	62	NJ83
Methven	52	NO02
Methwold	26	TL79
Mevagissey	4	SX04
Mexborough	36	SE40

Mey	67	ND27
Micheldever	10	SU53
Mickleton	24	SP14
Mid Yell	63	HU59
Middle Town	4	SV80
Middle Wallop	10	SU23
Middleham	40	SE18
Middlesbrough	40	NZ41
Middleton	35	SD80
Middleton	50	NL94
Middleton Stoney	16	SP52
Middleton-in-Teesdale	39	NY92
Middleton-on-Sea	11	SU90
Middleton-on-the-Wolds	36	SE94
Middlewich	30	SJ76
Midhurst	11	SU82
Midsomer Norton	15	ST65
Midtown Brae	59	NG88
Mildenhall	26	TL77
Milesmark	52	NT08
Milford	11	SU94
Milford Haven	20	SM90
Milford on Sea	10	SZ29
Millbrook	5	SX45
Millbrook	9	JS00
Millhouse	51	NR97
Milom	38	SD18
Milnathort	53	NO10
Milngavie	47	NS57
Milnrow	35	SD91
Milnthorpe	39	SD48
Milovaig	58	NG14
Milton	20	SN00
Milton Abbas	9	ST80
Milton Common	16	SP60
Milton Damerel	6	SS31
Milton Ernest	25	TL05
Milton Keynes	25	SP83
Milton on Stour	15	ST72
Minchinhampton	15	SO80
Minehead	7	SS94
Minera	29	SJ25
Minster	13	TR36
Minster Lovell	16	SP31
Minsterley	23	SJ30
Mintlaw	63	NJ94
Mirfield	35	SE21
Miskin	14	ST08
Misterton	36	SK79
Mitcham	17	TQ26
Mitcheldean	23	SO61
Mobberley	30	SJ77
Mochrum	42	NX34
Modbury	5	SX65
Moffat	43	NT00
Mold	29	SJ26
Moniaive	43	NX79
Monifieth	53	NO43
Monk Fryston	36	SE52
Monkleigh	6	SS42
Monmouth	23	SO51
Montacute	9	ST41
Montgomery	23	SO29
Montrose	53	NO75
Monymusk	57	NJ61
Morar	54	NM69
Morcott	25	SK90
Morden	17	TQ26
Mordiford	23	SO53
Morebattle	49	NT72
Morecambe	39	SD46
Moreton	34	SJ28
Moreton-in-Marsh	24	SP23
Moretonhampstead	8	SX78
Morfa Nefyn	28	SH24
Morley	35	SE22
Morningside	48	NT27
Morpeth	45	NZ18
Mortehoe	6	SS44
Morville	23	SO69
Morwenstow	6	SS21
Mossat	57	NJ41
Mossley	35	SD90
Mostyn	29	SJ18
Motherwell	47	NS75
Mottram in Longdendale	35	SJ99
Moulsford	16	SU58
Mount Hawke	4	SW74
Mountain Ash	14	ST09
Mountsorrel	32	SK51
Mousehole	4	SW42
Moy	60	NH73
Much Birch	23	SO53
Much Hadham	18	TL41
Much Hoole	34	SD42
Much Wenlock	23	SO69
Muchalls	57	NO99

Muddiford	6	SS53
Mudeford	10	SZ19
Muir of Ord	60	NH55
Muirdrum	53	NO53
Muirhead	47	NS66
Muirhead	53	NO33
Muirkirk	47	NS62
Mullion	4	SW61
Mullion Cove	4	SW61
Mundesley	27	TG33
Mundford	26	TL89
Mungrisdale	44	NY33
Munslow	23	SO58
Murton	45	NZ34
Musselburgh	48	NT37
Muthill	52	NN81
Mybster	67	ND15
Mytholmroyd	35	SE02

N

Nailsea	14	ST47
Nailsworth	15	ST89
Nairn	61	NH85
Nannerch	29	SJ16
Nant-ddu	22	SO01
Nantwich	30	SJ65
Narberth	20	SN11
Narborough	24	SP59
Narborough	26	TF71
Nayland	19	TL93
Neasham	40	NZ31
Neath	21	SS79
Needham Market	19	TM05
Nefyn	28	SH34
Nelson	35	SD83
Nesscliffe	30	SJ31
Neston	29	SJ27
Nether Broughton	32	SK62
Nether Stowey	14	ST13
Nether Wasdale	38	NY10
Nethy Bridge	56	NJ02
Nettlebed	16	SU68
Nevern	20	SN04
New Abbey	43	NX96
New Aberdour	62	NJ86
New Alresford	10	SU53
New Brighton	34	SJ39
New Buckenham	27	TM09
New Byth	62	NJ85
New Cumnock	47	NS61
New Deer	62	NJ84
New Galloway	43	NX67
New Grimsby	4	SV81
New Holland	37	TA02
New Luce	42	NX16
New Malden	17	TQ26
New Mills	31	SK08
New Milton	10	SZ29
New Pitsligo	62	NJ85
New Quay	21	SN35
New Radnor	22	SO26
New Romney	13	TR02
Newark-on-Trent	32	SK75
Newbiggin	39	NY92
Newbiggin-by-the-Sea	45	NZ38
Newbold on Stour	24	SP24
Newborough	28	SH46
Newbridge	48	NT17
Newbridge	16	SP40
Newbridge on Wye	22	SO05
Newburgh	53	NO21
Newburgh	63	NJ92
Newbury	35	SU46
Newby Bridge	39	SD38
Newcastle Emlyn	20	SN34
Newcastle upon Tyne	45	NZ26
Newcastle-under-Lyme	30	SJ84
Newcastleton	44	NY48
Newenden	13	TQ82
Newent	23	SO72
Newgale	20	SM82
Newgate Street	17	TL30
Newhaven	31	SK16
Newhaven	12	TQ40
Newhouse	47	NS76
Newlyn	4	SW42
Newmains	47	NS85
Newmarket	18	TL66
Newnham	15	SO61
Newnham	23	SO66
Newport	20	SN03

Newport	18	TL53
Newport	14	ST38
Newport	10	SZ58
Newport	30	SJ71
Newport Pagnell	25	SP84
Newport-on-Tay	53	NO42
Newquay	4	SW86
Newton Abbot	8	SX87
Newton Aycliffe	40	NZ22
Newton Ferrers	5	SX54
Newton on Trent	32	SK87
Newton Poppleford	8	SY08
Newton Solney	31	SK22
Newton St. Cyres	8	SX89
Newton Stewart	42	NX46
Newton Wamphray	43	NY19
Newton-le-Willows	34	SJ59
Newtonmore	56	NN79
Newtown	23	SO64
Newtown	22	SO19
Newtown Linford	32	SK50
Newtyle	53	NO24
Neyland	20	SM90
Nigg	61	NH87
Ninfield	12	TQ71
Niton	10	SZ57
Nolton Haven	20	SM81
Norden	35	SD81
Norham	49	NT94
Norman Cross	25	TL19
Normanton	32	SK90
Normanton	36	SE32
North Ballachulish	55	NN06
North Berwick	48	NT58
North Cotes	37	TA30
North Elmham	27	TF92
North Erradale	59	NG78
North Ferriby	37	SE92
North Grimston	41	SE86
North Kyme	33	TF15
North Molton	7	SS72
North Muskham	32	SK75
North Petherton	14	ST23
North Queensferry	48	NT18
North Shields	45	NZ36
North Somercotes	37	TF49
North Stifford	12	TQ68
North Tawton	6	SS60
North Walsham	27	TG23
North Waltham	10	SU54
North Wootton	14	ST54
Northallerton	40	SE39
Northam	6	SS42
Northampton	25	SP76
Northfleet	12	TQ67
Northiam	13	TQ82
Northleach	24	SP11
Northop	29	SJ26
Northop Hall	29	SJ26
Northwich	30	SJ67
Northwold	26	TL79
Northwood	17	TQ09
Norton	23	SJ70
Norton St. Philip	15	ST75
Norwich	27	TG20
Nottingham	32	SK53
Nuneaton	24	SP39
Nunney	15	ST74
Nutfield	12	TQ35
Nutley	12	TQ42

O

Oadby	25	SK60
Oakengates	30	SJ71
Oakham	32	SK80
Oakley	25	TL05
Oakley	16	SP61
Oakley	10	SU55
Oakworth	35	SE03
Oban	54	NM82
Ochiltree	47	NS52
Ockley	11	TQ14
Odiham	11	SU75
Ogbourne St. George	15	SU27
Ogmore-by-Sea	21	SS87
Okehampton	6	SX59
Old Deer	63	NJ94
Old Grimsby	4	SV81
Old Leake	33	TF45
Old Rayne	62	NJ62
Old Sodbury	15	ST78

Old Town	4	SV91
Old Windsor	17	SU97
Oldbury	24	SO98
Oldcotes	36	SK58
Oldham	35	SD90
Oldmeldrum	62	NJ82
Ollaberry	63	HU38
Olney	25	SP85
Ombersley	23	SO86
Onchan	38	SC37
Onich	55	NN06
Onneley	30	SJ74
Orford	19	TM45
Ormesby St. Michael	27	TG41
Ormskirk	34	SD40
Orpington	12	TQ46
Orsett	12	TQ68
Osbournby	33	TF03
Osmington	9	SY78
Ossett	35	SE22
Osterley	17	TQ17
Oswaldkirk	40	SE67
Oswaldtwistle	35	SD72
Oswestry	29	SJ22
Otford	12	TQ55
Othery	14	ST33
Otley	35	SE24
Otterburn	45	NY89
Ottershaw	17	TQ06
Ottery St. Mary	8	SY19
Oulton	36	SE32
Oulton Broad	27	TM59
Oundle	25	TL08
Outlane	35	SE01
Outwell	26	TF50
Over	30	SJ66
Overseal	31	SK21
Overstrand	27	TG24
Overton	30	SJ34
Overton	10	SU54
Oxenhope	35	SE03
Oxford	16	SP50
Oxted	12	TQ35
Oxton	32	SK65

P

Paddock Wood	12	TQ64
Padiham	35	SD73
Padstow	4	SW97
Padworth	16	SU66
Pagham	11	SZ89
Paignton	8	SX86
Painswick	15	SO80
Paisley	47	NS46
Pangbourne	16	SU67
Pannal	35	SE35
Pant-y-dwr	22	SN97
Papworth Everard	18	TL26
Par	5	SX05
Parbold	34	SD41
Parkeston Quay	19	TM23
Parkgate	29	SJ27
Parkham	6	SS32
Partick	47	NS56
Partington	34	SJ79
Partridge Green	11	TQ11
Pateley Bridge	40	SE16
Pathhead	48	NT36
Patrick	38	SC28
Patrington	37	TA32
Patterdale	39	NY31
Pattingham	23	SO89
Peacehaven	12	TQ40
Peasedown St. John	15	ST75
Peasmarsh	13	TQ82
Peat Inn	53	NO40
Peebles	48	NT24
Peel	38	SC28
Pelynt	5	SX25
Pembridge	23	SO35
Pembroke	20	SM90
Pembroke Dock	20	SM90
Pen-y-Bont-Fawr	29	SJ02
Pen-y-Gwryd Hotel	28	SH65
Penarth	14	ST17
Pencaitland	48	NT46
Pencoed	21	SS98
Pencraig	23	SO52
Pendeen	4	SW33
Pendine	20	SN20
Pendlebury	35	SD70

Pendoggett	4	SX07
Penicuik	48	NT25
Penistone	35	SE20
Penketh	34	SJ58
Penkridge	30	SJ91
Penmachno	29	SH75
Penmaen	21	SS58
Penmaenmawr	28	SH77
Pennal	22	SH60
Pennard	21	SS58
Pennyghael	50	NM52
Penrhyndeudraeth	28	SH63
Penrith	44	NY53
Penryn	4	SW73
Penshurst	12	TQ54
Pentewan	4	SX04
Pentre Llanrhaeadr	29	SJ06
Pentrefoelas	29	SH85
Penybont	22	SO16
Penygroes	28	SH45
Penzance	4	SW43
Perelle	4	GN00
Perivale	17	TQ18
Perranporth	4	SW75
Perranuthnoe	4	SW52
Perry Barr	24	SP09
Pershore	24	SO94
Perth	52	NO12
Peterborough	25	TL19
Peterchurch	23	SO33
Peterculter	57	NJ80
Peterhead	63	NK14
Peterlee	45	NZ44
Petersfield	11	SU72
Petts Wood	12	TQ46
Petty France	15	ST78
Petworth	11	SU92
Pevensey	12	TQ60
Pewsey	15	SU16
Pickering	41	SE78
Picket Post	10	SU10
Pickhill	40	SE38
Piddletrenthide	9	SY79
Piercebridge	40	NZ21
Pierowall	67	HY44
Pillerton Priors	24	SP24
Pilning	14	ST58
Pinchbeck	33	TF22
Pinner	17	TQ18
Pinwherry	42	NX28
Pirnmill	46	NR84
Pitcaple	62	NJ72
Pitlochry	52	NN95
Pitmedden	62	NJ82
Pitsea	18	TQ78
Pittenweem	53	NO50
Pleasley	32	SK56
Plemont	9	JS00
Plockton	59	NG83
Plymouth	5	SX45
Plympton	5	SX55
Pocklington	36	SE84
Podimore	14	ST52
Polbain	64	NB91
Polegate	12	TQ50
Polmont	52	NS97
Polperro	5	SX25
Polruan	5	SX15
Polzeath	4	SW97
Ponders End	17	TQ39
Pontardawe	21	SN70
Pontardulais	21	SN50
Pontefract	36	SE42
Ponteland	45	NZ17
Ponterwyd	22	SN78
Pontesbury	30	SJ30
Pontllanfraith	14	ST19
Pontnewydd	14	ST29
Pontrhydfendigaid	22	SN76
Pontrilas	23	SO32
Pontyates	21	SN40
Pontypool	14	SO20
Pontypridd	14	ST08
Pool	35	SZ09
Poole	10	SZ09
Poolewe	59	NG88
Pooley Bridge	39	NY42
Porlock	7	SS84
Porlock Weir	7	SS84
Port Appin	54	NM94
Port Askaig	50	NR46
Port Charlotte	50	NR25
Port Einon	21	SS48
Port Ellen	50	NR34
Port Erin	38	SC16
Port Gaverne	4	SX08
Port Glasgow	51	NS37

Port Henderson	59	NG77
Port Isaac	4	SW98
Port Logan	42	NX04
Port Nis	64	NB56
Port of Menteith	52	NN50
Port of Ness	64	NB56
Port Soderick	38	SC37
Port St. Mary	38	SC26
Port Talbot	21	SS78
Port William	42	NX34
Portavadie	51	NR96
Portchester	10	SU60
Porth	14	ST09
Porthallow	5	SX25
Porthcawl	21	SS87
Porthcurno	4	SW32
Porthkerry	7	ST06
Porthleven	4	SW62
Porthmadog	28	SH53
Porthtowan	4	SW64
Porthyrhyd	21	SN51
Portishead	14	ST47
Portknockie	62	NJ46
Portlethen	57	NO99
Portloe	4	SW93
Portmahomack	61	NH98
Portnacroish	55	NM94
Portnahaven	50	NR15
Portpatrick	42	NW95
Portreath	4	SW64
Portree	58	NG44
Portscatho	4	SW83
Portslade-by-Sea	12	TQ20
Portsmouth	11	SU60
Portsoy	62	NJ56
Postcombe	16	SP70
Pott Shrigley	31	SJ97
Potter Heigham	27	TG41
Potters Bar	17	TL20
Potton	18	TL24
Poulton-le-Fylde	34	SD33
Poundsgate	8	SX77
Powburn	49	NU01
Powfoot	43	NY16
Powick	23	SO85
Powmill	52	NT09
Poynton	30	SJ98
Praa Sands	4	SW52
Praze-an-Beeble	4	SW63
Preesall	34	SD34
Prenteg	28	SH54
Prescot	34	SJ49
Prestatyn	29	SJ08
Prestbury	30	SJ87
Presteigne	23	SO36
Preston	49	NT75
Preston	34	SD52
Preston Gubbals	30	SJ41
Prestwich	35	SD80
Prestwick	47	NS32
Princes Risborough	16	SP80
Princethorpe	24	SP47
Princetown	5	SX57
Prudhoe	45	NZ06
Puckeridge	18	TL32
Puddington	29	SJ37
Puddletown	9	SY79
Pudsey	35	SE23
Pulborough	11	TQ01
Pumsaint	21	SN64
Purfleet	12	TQ57
Purley	12	TQ36
Purton	15	SU08
Pwllheli	28	SH33
Pyle	21	SS88

Queenborough	13	TQ97
Queensbury	35	SE13
Queensferry	29	SJ36
Quendon	18	TL53
Quorndon	32	SK51

Radcliffe	35	SD70

Radcliffe on Trent	32	SK63
Radlett	17	TL10
Radstock	15	ST65
Radwinter	18	TL63
Rafford	61	NJ05
Raglan	14	SO40
Rainford	34	SD40
Rainham	12	TQ58
Rainhill	34	SJ49
Rame	4	SW73
Ramsbottom	35	SD71
Ramsey	26	TL28
Ramsey	38	SC49
Ramsgate	13	TR36
Ramsgill	40	SE17
Rangeworthy	15	ST68
Rannoch Station	55	NN45
Ranworth	27	TG31
Rapness	67	HY54
Rattray	53	NO14
Ravenglass	38	SD09
Ravenscar	40	NZ90
Ravenstonedale	39	NY70
Rawmarsh	36	SK49
Rawtenstall	35	SD82
Rayleigh	18	TQ89
Read	35	SD73
Reading	16	SU77
Rearsby	32	SK61
Reay	66	NC96
Red Row	45	NZ29
Redbourn	17	TL11
Redbrook	30	SJ54
Redcar	40	NZ62
Redditch	24	SP06
Redhill	12	TQ25
Redland	67	HY32
Redmile	32	SK73
Redruth	4	SW64
Reedham	27	TG40
Reepham	27	TG12
Reeth	40	SE09
Reiff	64	NB91
Reigate	12	TQ25
Reighton	41	TA17
Rempstone	32	SK52
Renfrew	47	NS56
Renishaw	31	SK47
Resolven	21	SN80
Retford	32	SK78
Rettendon	18	TQ79
Reynoldston	21	SS48
Rhayader	22	SN96
Rhiconich	65	NC25
Rhoose	7	ST06
Rhos	21	SN33
Rhos-on-Sea	29	SH88
Rhosneigr	28	SH37
Rhossili	21	SS48
Rhu	51	NS28
Rhubodach	51	NS07
Rhuddlan	29	SJ07
Rhyd-Ddu	28	SH55
Rhydowen	21	SN44
Rhyl	29	SJ08
Rhymney	14	SO10
Rhynie	62	NJ42
Ribchester	34	SD63
Richards Castle	23	SO46
Richmond	40	NZ10
Richmond upon Thames	17	TQ17
Rickmansworth	17	TQ09
Ridsdale	45	NY98
Rillington	41	SE87
Ringford	43	NX65
Ringshall	17	SP91
Ringwood	10	SU10
Ripley	31	SK35
Ripley	40	SE26
Ripley	17	TQ05
Ripon	40	SE37
Ripple	23	SO83
Ripponden	35	SE01
Risca	14	ST29
Risegate	33	TF22
Riseley	25	TL06
Rishton	34	SD73
Risley	31	SK43
Road Weedon	25	SP65
Roadhead	44	NY57
Roberton	47	NS92
Robertsbridge	12	TQ72
Robeston Wathen	20	SN01
Robin Hood's Bay	41	NZ90
Rocester	31	SK13
Rochdale	35	SD81
Rochester	12	TQ76

Rochester	44	NY89
Rochford	19	TQ89
Rock	4	SW97
Rock Ferry	34	SJ38
Rockcliffe	43	NX85
Rockingham	25	SP89
Rogart	66	NC70
Rogerstone	14	ST28
Rolvenden	13	TQ83
Romaldkirk	39	NY92
Romford	18	TQ58
Romsey	10	SU32
Romsley	24	SO98
Rookhope	45	NY94
Ropley	11	SU63
Rosebank	47	NS84
Rosedale Abbey	41	SE79
Rosehall	65	NC40
Rosehearty	63	NJ96
Rosemarkie	60	NH75
Roslin	48	NT26
Ross-on-Wye	23	SO52
Rossett	30	SJ35
Rossington	36	SK69
Rosthwaite	38	NY21
Rosyth	48	NT18
Rothbury	45	NU00
Rotherham	36	SK49
Rotherwick	16	SU75
Rothes	61	NJ24
Rothesay	51	NS06
Rothley	32	SK51
Rothwell	25	SP88
Rothwell	35	SE32
Rottingdean	12	TQ30
Roughton	27	TG23
Rousdon	8	SY29
Rowardennan Lodge	51	NS39
Rowen	28	SH77
Rowland's Castle	11	SU71
Rowland's Gill	45	NZ15
Rowley Regis	24	SO98
Rowsley	31	SK26
Rowstock	16	SU48
Roxburgh	49	NT63
Roy Bridge	55	NN28
Royston	18	TL34
Royston	36	SE31
Royton	35	SD90
Rozel	9	JS00
Ruabon	29	SJ34
Ruan High Lanes	4	SW93
Ruan Minor	4	SW71
Rubery	24	SO97
Rudgwick	11	TQ03
Rudston	41	TA06
Rufford	34	SD41
Rugby	24	SP57
Rugeley	31	SK01
Ruislip	17	TQ08
Rumney	14	ST27
Runcorn	30	SJ58
Rushden	25	SP96
Rushyford	40	NZ22
Rusper	11	TQ23
Rustington	11	TQ00
Ruswarp	41	NZ80
Rutherglen	47	NS66
Ruthin	29	SJ15
Ruyton-XI-Towns	30	SJ32
Ryde	10	SZ59
Rye	13	TQ92
Ryhope	45	NZ45
Ryton	45	NZ16

Sacriston	45	NZ24
Sadberge	40	NZ31
Saddell	46	NR73
Saffron Walden	18	TL53
St Abbs	49	NT96
St Agnes	4	SW75
St Albans	17	TL10
St Andrew	17	GN00
St Andrews	53	NO51
St Anne's	34	SD32
St Arvans	14	ST59
St Asaph	29	SJ07
St Aubin	9	JS00
St Austell	4	SX05
St Bees	38	NX91

St Blazey	5	SX05
St Boswells	48	NT53
St Brelade	9	JS00
St Brelades Bay	9	JS00
St Brides	20	SM81
St Clears	20	SN21
St Cleer	5	SX26
St Clement	9	JS00
St Combs	63	NK06
St Cyrus	57	NO76
St Davids	20	SM72
St Day	4	SW74
St Dogmaels	20	SN14
St Fergus	63	NK05
St Fillans	52	NN62
St Helens	11	SZ68
St Helens	34	SJ59
St Helier	9	JS00
St Ives	26	TL37
St Ives	4	SW54
St John	9	JS00
St John's	38	SC28
St John's Chapel	45	NY83
St John's Town of Dalry	43	NX68
St Jude's	38	SC39
St Just	4	SW33
St Keverne	4	SW72
St Lawrence	10	SZ57
St Lawrence	9	JS00
St Leonards	10	SU10
St Leonards	12	TQ80
St Margaret's at Cliffe	13	TR34
St Margarets Hope	67	ND49
St Marks	38	SC27
St Martin	9	GN00
St Martin	9	JS00
St Mary	9	JS00
St Mary's	67	HY40
St Mary's Bay	13	TR02
St Marychurch	8	SX96
St Mawes	4	SW83
St Mawgan	4	SW86
St Mellion	5	SX36
St Michael's on Wyre	34	SD44
St Monans	53	NO50
St Neot	5	SX16
St Neots	25	TL16
St Ouen	9	JS00
St Peter	9	JS00
St Peter Port	9	GN00
St Peter's	9	GN00
St Sampson	9	GN00
St Saviour	9	JS00
St Teath	5	SX08
Salcombe	8	SX73
Sale	35	SJ79
Salen	54	NM66
Salford	35	SJ89
Saline	52	NT09
Salisbury	10	SU12
Saltash	5	SX45
Saltburn-by-the-Sea	40	NZ62
Saltcoats	46	NS24
Saltfleet	37	TF49
Salthouse	27	TG04
Sampford Peverell	7	ST01
Sandbach	30	SJ76
Sandbanks	10	SZ08
Sanderstead	12	TQ36
Sandford	14	ST45
Sandhaven	63	NJ96
Sandhead	42	NX04
Sandhurst	16	SU86
Sandiacre	32	SK43
Sandiway	30	SJ67
Sandness	63	HU15
Sandown	10	SZ58
Sandringham	26	TF62
Sandsend	41	NZ81
Sandwich	13	TR35
Sandy	25	TL14
Sanquhar	47	NS70
Sarisbury	10	SU50
Sarn	28	SH23
Sarnesfield	23	SO35
Sarre	13	TR26
Saul	15	SO70
Saundersfoot	20	SN10
Saunderton	16	SP70
Saunton	6	SS43
Sawbridgeworth	18	TL41
Sawley	35	SD74
Sawston	18	TL44
Saxby	32	SK81
Saxmundham	19	TM36
Saxthorpe	27	TG13
Scalasaig	50	NR39
Scalby	41	TA09
Scalloway	63	HU43
Scarborough	41	TA08
Scarinish	50	NM04
Scarisbrick	34	SD31
Scawby	36	SE90
Scole	27	TM17
Sconser	58	NG53
Scopwick	33	TF05
Scorton	40	NZ20
Scotch Corner	40	NZ20
Scourie	65	NC14
Scrabster	67	ND17
Scunthorpe	36	SE81
Sea Palling	27	TG42
Seaford	12	TV49
Seaham	45	NZ44
Seahouses	49	NU23
Seamer	41	TA08
Seamill	46	NS24
Seascale	38	NY00
Seathwaite	38	SD29
Seatoller	38	NY21
Seaton	8	SY29
Seaton Burn	45	NZ27
Seaton Carew	40	NZ52
Seaview	11	SZ69
Sedbergh	39	SD69
Sedgeberrow	24	SP03
Sedgebrook	32	SK83
Sedgefield	40	NZ32
Sedgley	24	SO99
Sedlescombe	12	TQ71
Selborne	11	SU73
Selby	36	SE63
Selkirk	48	NT42
Selly Oak	24	SP08
Selsey	11	SZ89
Senghenydd	14	ST19
Sennen	4	SW32
Sennybridge	22	SN92
Settle	39	SD86
Sevenoaks	12	TQ55
Severn Stoke	23	SO84
Shaftesbury	15	ST82
Shaldon	8	SX97
Shalfleet	10	SZ48
Shandon	51	NS28
Shanklin	10	SZ58
Shap	39	NY51
Shardlow	31	SK43
Sharnbrook	25	SP95
Sharnford	24	SP49
Sharpness	15	SO60
Shaw	35	SD90
Shawbury	30	SJ52
Shawell	24	SP58
Shedfield	10	SU51
Sheerness	13	TQ97
Sheffield	31	SK38
Shefford	25	TL13
Sheldon	24	SP18
Shelf	35	SE12
Shenstone	24	SK10
Shepley	35	SE10
Shepperton	17	TQ06
Shepreth	18	TL34
Shepshed	32	SK41
Shepton Mallet	15	ST64
Sheraton	45	NZ43
Sherborne	9	ST61
Sherburn	41	SE97
Sherburn in Elmet	36	SE43
Sherfield on Loddon	16	SU65
Sheriff Hutton	40	SE66
Sheringham	27	TG14
Sherston	15	ST88
Shevington	34	SD50
Shiel Bridge	59	NG91
Shieldaig	59	NG85
Shifnal	30	SJ70
Shildon	40	NZ22
Shillingford	16	SU59
Shipdham	27	TF90
Shipham	14	ST45
Shiplake	16	SU77
Shipley	35	SE13
Shipston on Stour	24	SP24
Shipton-under-Wychwood	16	SP21
Shiptonthorpe	36	SE84
Shirley	24	SP17
Shoeburyness	19	TQ98
Shoreham-by-Sea	11	TQ20
Shorwell	10	SZ48
Shotley	19	TM23
Shottisham	19	TM34
Shrawley	23	SO86
Shrewsbury	30	SJ41
Shrewton	15	SU04
Shrivenham	15	SU28
Shurdington	24	SO91
Sible Hedingham	18	TL73
Sibsey	33	TF35
Sibson	24	SK30
Sidcup	12	TQ47
Sidmouth	8	SY18
Silchester	16	SU66
Silloth	43	NY15
Silver End	18	TL81
Silverdale	39	SD47
Silverstone	25	SP64
Simonsbath	7	SS73
Singleton	11	SU81
Sittingbourne	13	TQ96
Six Mile Bottom	18	TL55
Skaill	67	HY50
Skeabost	58	NG44
Skegness	33	TF56
Skellow	36	SE51
Skelmersdale	34	SD40
Skelmorlie	51	NS16
Skenfrith	23	SO42
Skipness	46	NR95
Skipsea	41	TA15
Skipton	35	SD95
Slaidburn	34	SD75
Slaithwaite	35	SE01
Slamannan	47	NS87
Slapton	8	SX84
Sleaford	33	TF04
Sledmere	41	SE96
Sliddery	46	NR92
Sligachan	58	NG42
Slimbridge	15	SO70
Slough	17	SU97
Smailholm	49	NT63
Small Dole	11	TQ21
Smallways	40	NZ11
Smethwick	24	SP08
Snaith	36	SE62
Snake Pass Inn	35	SK19
Snarestone	31	SK30
Snettisham	26	TF63
Solihull	24	SP17
Somersham	26	TL37
Somerton	14	ST42
Sonning	16	SU77
Sorbie	42	NX44
Sorisdale	50	NM26
Sorn	47	NS52
Soulby	39	NY71
Sourton	5	SX59
South Benfleet	18	TQ78
South Brent	8	SX66
South Cave	36	SE93
South Godstone	12	TQ34
South Harting	11	SU71
South Milton	8	SX74
South Mimms	17	TL20
South Molton	6	SS72
South Normanton	31	SK45
South Petherton	9	ST41
South Queensferry	48	NT17
South Raynham	26	TF82
South Shields	45	NZ36
South Walsham	27	TG31
South Wigston	25	SP59
South Witham	32	SK91
South Woodham Ferrers	18	TQ89
South Zeal	5	SX69
Southall	17	TQ17
Southam	24	SP46
Southampton	10	SU41
Southborough	12	TQ54
Southend-on-Sea	19	TQ88
Southgate	17	TQ29
Southminster	19	TQ99
Southmoor	16	SU39
Southport	34	SD31
Southrepps	27	TG23
Southsea	11	SZ69
Southwell	32	SK65
Southwold	27	TM57
Sowerby Bridge	35	SE02
Spalding	33	TF22
Sparkford	15	ST62
Spean Bridge	55	NN28
Speke	30	SJ48
Spencers Wood	16	SU76
Spennymoor	45	NZ23
Spey Bay	62	NJ36
Spilsby	33	TF46
Spittal of Glenshee	56	NO17
Spratton	25	SP76

Stadhampton	16	SU69
Stadhlaigearraidh	64	NF73
Staffin	58	NG46
Stafford	30	SJ92
Staindrop	40	NZ12
Staines	17	TQ07
Stainforth	39	SD86
Staithes	41	NZ71
Stalham	27	TG32
Stallingborough	37	TA11
Stalybridge	35	SJ99
Stamford	33	TF00
Stamford Bridge	41	SE75
Standish	34	SD51
Standlake	16	SP30
Stanhope	45	NY93
Stanley	45	NZ15
Stanley	52	NO13
Stanmore	17	TQ19
Stanstead Abbots	18	TL31
Stansted Mountfitchet	18	TL52
Stanton	27	TL97
Stanton Harcourt	16	SP40
Stanway	24	SP03
Stapleford	32	SK43
Staplehurst	12	TQ74
Starcross	8	SX98
Staveley	31	SK47
Staverton	8	SX76
Staxton	41	TA07
Steeple Aston	24	SP42
Steeple Bumpstead	18	TL64
Steeton	35	SE04
Stein	58	NG25
Steornabhagh	64	NB43
Stepaside	20	SN10
Stepps	47	NS66
Stevenage	17	TL22
Stevenston	46	NS24
Stewarton	47	NS44
Steyning	11	TQ11
Stibb Cross	6	SS41
Stickney	33	TF35
Stilligarry	64	NF73
Stillington	40	SE56
Stilton	25	TL18
Stirling	52	NS79
Stockbridge	10	SU33
Stockport	35	SJ89
Stocksbridge	35	SK29
Stockton Heath	30	SJ68
Stockton-on-Tees	40	NZ41
Stoer	64	NC02
Stogursey	14	ST24
Stoke Canon	8	SX99
Stoke D'Abernon	17	TQ15
Stoke Ferry	26	TF70
Stoke Fleming	8	SX84
Stoke Gabriel	8	SX85
Stoke Goldington	25	SP84
Stoke Mandeville	16	SP81
Stoke-by-Nayland	19	TL93
Stoke-on-Trent (Hanley)	30	SJ84
Stokenchurch	16	SU79
Stokesley	40	NZ50
Ston Easton	15	ST65
Stone	30	SJ93
Stonehaven	57	NO88
Stonehouse	15	SO80
Stoneykirk	42	NX05
Stonor	16	SU78
Stornoway	64	NB43
Storrington	11	TQ01
Stotfold	18	TL23
Stourbridge	24	SO88
Stourport-on-Severn	23	SO87
Stourton	23	SO88
Stow	48	NT44
Stow-on-the-Wold	24	SP12
Stowmarket	19	TM05
Strachan	57	NO69
Strachur	51	NN00
Stradbroke	27	TM27
Stradishall	18	TL75
Stradsett	26	TF60
Straiton	47	NS30
Stranraer	42	NX06
Stratfield Turgis	16	SU65
Stratford	18	TQ38
Stratford-upon-Avon	24	SP25
Strathaven	47	NS74
Strathblane	52	NS57
Strathcarron Sta.	59	NG94
Strathdon	57	NJ31
Strathkanaird	65	NC10
Strathmiglo	53	NO20
Strathpeffer	60	NH45

Strathy	66	NC86
Strathyre	52	NN51
Stratton	6	SS20
Streatham	17	TQ37
Streatley	16	SU58
Street	14	ST43
Strensall	40	SE66
Strete	8	SX84
Stretford	35	SJ79
Stretham	26	TL57
Stretton	30	SJ68
Stretton	32	SK91
Strichen	63	NJ95
Stromeferry	59	NG83
Stromness	67	HY20
Stronachlachar	51	NN41
Strone	51	NS18
Strontian	54	NM86
Strood	12	TQ76
Stroud	15	SO80
Struan	58	NG33
Struy	60	NH44
Studland	10	SZ08
Studley	24	SP06
Sturminster Newton	9	ST71
Sturton by Stow	32	SK88
Sudbury	31	SK13
Sudbury	19	TL84
Sulby	38	SC39
Sullom Voe	63	HU47
Summercourt	4	SW85
Sunbury	17	TQ16
Sunderland	45	NZ35
Surbiton	17	TQ16
Sutterton	33	TF23
Sutton	12	TQ26
Sutton Benger	15	ST97
Sutton Coldfield	24	SP19
Sutton in Ashfield	32	SK45
Sutton in the Elms	24	SP59
Sutton on Sea	33	TF58
Sutton on Trent	32	SK76
Sutton Scotney	10	SU43
Sutton upon Derwent	36	SE74
Sutton Valence	12	TQ84
Sutton-on-the-Forest	40	SE56
Swadlincote	31	SK21
Swaffham	26	TF80
Swainswick	15	ST76
Swalcliffe	24	SP33
Swallowfield	16	SU76
Swanage	10	SZ07
Swanley	12	TQ56
Swansea	21	SS69
Swavesey	18	TL36
Sway	10	SZ29
Swaythling	10	SU41
Swillington	36	SE33
Swindon	15	SU18
Swineshead	25	TL06
Swineshead	33	TF24
Swinton	9	NT84
Swinton	36	SK49
Syderstone	26	TF83
Symbister	63	HU56
Symington	48	NS93
Symonds Yat	23	SO51
Synod Inn	21	SN45
Syre	66	NC64
Syston	32	SK61

Taplow	16	SU98
Tarbert	51	NR86
Tarbert	64	NB10
Tarbet	51	NN30
Tarbolton	47	NS42
Tarfside	57	NO47
Tarland	57	NJ40
Tarleton	34	SD42
Tarporley	30	SJ56
Tarskavaig	58	NG51
Tarves	62	NJ83
Taunton	14	ST22
Tavistock	5	SX47
Tayinloan	46	NR64
Taynuilt	55	NN03
Tayport	53	NO42
Tayvallich	50	NR78
Teangue	58	NG60
Tedburn St. Mary	8	SX89
Teddington	17	TQ17
Teignmouth	8	SX97
Telford	30	SJ60
Temple	48	NT35
Temple Bar	21	SN55
Temple Ewell	13	TR24
Temple Sowerby	39	NY62
Templecombe	15	ST72
Templeton	20	SN11
Tenbury Wells	23	SO56
Tenby	20	SN10
Tenterden	13	TQ83
Ternhill	30	SJ63
Tetbury	15	ST89
Tetford	33	TF37
Teviothead	44	NT40
Tewkesbury	23	SO83
Thakeham	11	TQ11
Thame	16	SP70
Thames Ditton	17	TQ16
Thatcham	16	SU56
Thaxted	18	TL63
The Bungalow	38	SC38
The Mumbles	21	SS68
Theale	16	SU67
Thetford	26	TL88
Theydon Bois	18	TQ49
Thirlspot	38	NY31
Thirsk	40	SE48
Thornaby-on-Tees	40	NZ41
Thornbury	15	ST69
Thorne	36	SE61
Thorney	26	TF20
Thornhill	52	NN60
Thornhill	43	NX89
Thornley	45	NZ33
Thornthwaite	38	NY22
Thornton	34	SD34
Thornton	34	SD30
Thornton Dale	41	SE88
Thornton Heath	17	TQ36
Thornton Hough	29	SJ38
Thornton Watlass	40	SE28
Thornton-le-Street	40	SE48
Thorpe	31	SK15
Thorpe Bay	13	TQ98
Thorpe Market	27	TG23
Thorpe Thewles	40	NZ32
Thorpe-le-Soken	19	TM12
Thorpeness	19	TM45
Thorverton	7	SS90
Thrapston	25	SP97
Three Cocks	22	SO13
Threekingham	33	TF03
Threshfield	39	SD96
Thropton	45	NU00
Throwleigh	5	SX69
Thrumster	67	ND34
Thrussington	32	SK61
Thurcroft	36	SK48
Thurlaston	24	SP47
Thurlestone	5	SX64
Thurmaston	32	SK60
Thurnby	25	SK60
Thurnscoe	36	SE40
Thursby	44	NY35
Thurso	67	ND16
Thwaite	39	SD89
Ticehurst	12	TQ63
Tickhill	36	SK59
Ticknall	31	SK32
Tideford	5	SX35
Tideswell	31	SK17
Tigh a Ghearraidh	64	NF77
Tigharry	64	NF77
Tighnabruaich	51	NR97
Tilbury	12	TQ67
Tilford	11	SU84

Tillicoultry 52 NS99
Tilshead.................... 15 SU04
Tilton on the Hill......... 32 SK70
Timperley 35 SJ78
Tintagel 5 SX08
Tintern Parva.............. 14 SO50
Tintwistle................. 35 SK09
Tipton...................... 24 SO99
Tiptree 19 TL81
Titchwell.................. 26 TF74
Tiverton.................... 7 SS91
Tobermory 54 NM55
Toddington................ 25 TL02
Todmorden............... 35 SD92
Todwick................... 32 SK48
Tolastadh.................. 64 NB54
Tollesbury................ 19 TL91
Tolleshunt D'Arcy....... 19 TL91
Tolleshunt Knights...... 19 TL91
Tolsta...................... 64 NB54
Tolworth.................. 17 TQ16
Tomatin................... 61 NH82
Tomdoun.................. 55 NH10
Tomich.................... 60 NH32
Tomintoul................. 56 NJ11
Tomnavoulin.............. 61 NJ22
Tonbridge................. 12 TQ54
Tongue.................... 66 NC55
Tonypandy 14 SS99
Tonyrefail................. 14 ST08
Topcliffe.................. 40 SE37
Topsham................... 8 SX98
Torcross.................... 8 SX84
Tore....................... 60 NH65
Tormarton................. 15 ST77
Torness.................... 60 NH52
Torphins................... 57 NJ60
Torpoint.................... 5 SX45
Torquay.................... 8 SX96
Torrance.................. 47 NS67
Torridon.................. 59 NG95
Torrin..................... 58 NG52
Torthorwald.............. 43 NY07
Torver..................... 38 SD29
Totland.................... 10 SZ38
Totnes...................... 8 SX86
Tottington................ 35 SD71
Totton..................... 10 SU31
Tow Law.................. 45 NZ13
Towcester................ 25 SP64
Town Yetholm........... 49 NT82
Tranent................... 48 NT47
Tranmere................. 29 SJ38
Traquair................... 48 NT33
Trawsfynydd............. 28 SH73
Trearddur Bay........... 28 SH27
Trebetherick.............. 4 SW97
Trecastle.................. 22 SN82
Tredegar.................. 14 SO10
Trefriw................... 29 SH76
Tregaron.................. 21 SN65
Tregony.................... 4 SW94
Tregurrian................. 4 SW86
Treherbert................ 21 SS99
Trelleck................... 14 SO50
Tremadog................. 28 SH54
Treyarnon.................. 4 SW87
Trimdon................... 45 NZ33
Trimingham............... 27 TG23
Tring...................... 17 SP91
Trinity..................... 9 JS00
Troon...................... 47 NS33
Troutbeck................ 39 NY40
Trowbridge............... 15 ST85
Truro....................... 4 SW84
Tummel Bridge.......... 52 NN75
Tunbridge Wells......... 12 TQ53
Tunstall................... 19 TM35
Turnberry................. 46 NS20
Turner's Hill.............. 12 TQ33
Turriff..................... 62 NJ75
Turton Bottoms.......... 35 SD71
Turvey.................... 25 SP95
Tutbury................... 31 SK22
Tuxford................... 32 SK77
Tweedsmuir.............. 48 NT12
Twickenham.............. 17 TQ17
Two Bridges............... 5 SX67
Twycross.................. 31 SK30
Twyford................... 16 SU77
Twyford................... 10 SU42
Tyldesley................. 34 SD60
Tyndrum.................. 55 NN33
Tynemouth............... 45 NZ36
Tywyn..................... 22 SH50

Ubley...................... 14 ST55
Uckfield................... 12 TQ42
Uddingston............... 47 NS66
Uffculme................... 7 ST01
Uig........................ 58 NG36
Uig........................ 64 NB03
Ulceby.................... 33 TF47
Uldale..................... 44 NY23
Ullapool................... 65 NH19
Ullesthorpe............... 24 SP58
Ullingswick............... 23 SO54
Ulpha..................... 38 SD19
Ulsta...................... 63 HU48
Ulverston................. 38 SD27
Umberleigh................. 6 SS62
Unapool................... 65 NC23
Union Mills............... 38 SC37
Up Holland............... 34 SD50
Upavon.................... 15 SU15
Uphall.................... 48 NT07
Upminster................ 18 TQ58
Upottery................... 8 ST20
Upper Breakish.......... 59 NG62
Upper Broughton........ 32 SK62
Upper Largo.............. 53 NO40
Upper Slaughter......... 24 SP12
Uppermill................. 35 SD90
Uppingham............... 25 SP89
Upton...................... 36 SE41
Upton upon Severn..... 23 SO84
Urmston................... 35 SJ79
Usk....................... 14 SO30
Uttoxeter................. 31 SK03
Uxbridge................. 17 TQ08

Vale........................ 9 GN00
Valley..................... 28 SH27
Vazon Bay.................. 9 GN00
Ventnor................... 10 SZ57
Verwood.................. 10 SU00
Veryan..................... 4 SW93
Vickerstown.............. 38 SD16
Voe....................... 63 HU46

Waddington.............. 35 SD74
Waddington.............. 32 SK96
Wadebridge................ 4 SW97
Wadhurst.................. 12 TQ63
Wainfleet All Saints..... 33 TF45
Wakefield................. 35 SE32
Walkden.................. 35 SD70
Walkerburn............... 48 NT33
Walkington............... 37 SE93
Wall....................... 45 NY96
Wallasey.................. 34 SJ29
Wallingford............... 16 SU68
Wallington............... 17 TQ26
Walls..................... 63 HU24
Wallsend.................. 45 NZ26
Wallyford................. 48 NT37
Walmer.................... 13 TR35
Walsall.................... 24 SP09
Walsden.................. 35 SD92
Walterstone.............. 23 SO32
Waltham.................. 37 TA20
Waltham Abbey......... 18 TL30
Waltham on the Wolds.. 32 SK82
Walthamstow............ 17 TQ38
Walton.................... 23 SO25
Walton on the Naze..... 19 TM22
Walton-on-Thames...... 17 TQ16
Wandsworth.............. 17 TQ27
Wanlockhead............. 47 NS81
Wansford................. 25 TL09
Wantage.................. 16 SU38
Warboys.................. 26 TL38
Warburton................ 34 SJ78

Warcop................... 39 NY71
Ware...................... 17 TL31
Wareham................... 9 SY98
Wargrave.................. 16 SU77
Wark...................... 44 NY87
Warkworth................ 45 NU20
Warmington.............. 24 SP44
Warminster............... 15 ST84
Warmley.................. 15 ST67
Warmsworth.............. 36 SE50
Warrington............... 34 SJ68
Warsash................... 10 SU40
Warsop.................... 32 SK56
Warton.................... 34 SD42
Warwick................... 24 SP26
Wasdale Head............ 38 NY10
Washington............... 45 NZ35
Watchet.................... 7 ST04
Waterbeach............... 11 SU80
Waterhouses............. 31 SK05
Wateringbury............ 12 TQ65
Waterlooville............. 11 SU60
Watermillock............. 39 NY42
Watford................... 17 TQ19
Wath upon Dearne...... 36 SE40
Watlington............... 16 SU69
Watten.................... 67 ND25
Watton.................... 26 TF90
Watton-at-Stone........ 17 TL31
Wealdstone.............. 17 TQ18
Wear Head............... 44 NY83
Weaverham.............. 30 SJ67
Wedmore.................. 14 ST44
Wednesbury.............. 24 SO99
Welford................... 25 SP68
Wellesbourne............ 24 SP25
Welling................... 12 TQ47
Wellingborough......... 25 SP86
Wellington................ 30 SJ61
Wellington................. 7 ST12
Wells..................... 14 ST54
Wells-Next-The-Sea.... 26 TF94
Welney.................... 26 TL59
Welshampton............ 30 SJ43
Welshpool................ 29 SJ20
Welwyn Garden City.... 17 TL21
Wem...................... 30 SJ52
Wembley.................. 17 TQ18
Wembury................... 5 SX54
Wemyss Bay.............. 51 NS16
Wendover................. 16 SP80
Wensley.................. 40 SE08
Wentbridge.............. 36 SE41
Weobley.................. 23 SO45
West Auckland.......... 40 NZ12
West Bexington.......... 9 SY58
West Bilney.............. 26 TF71
West Bromwich......... 24 SP09
West Byfleet............. 17 TQ06
West Calder............. 48 NT06
West Chiltington........ 11 TQ01
West Coker................ 9 ST51
West Drayton............ 17 TQ07
West Haddon............. 25 SP67
West Harptree........... 14 ST55
West Horsley............. 11 TQ05
West Kilbride............ 46 NS24
West Kirby............... 29 SJ28
West Lavington.......... 15 SU05
West Linton.............. 48 NT15
West Lulworth............ 9 SY88
West Meon............... 11 SU62
West Mersea............. 19 TM01
West Molesey............ 17 TQ16
West Pentire.............. 4 SW76
West Quantoxhead....... 7 ST14
West Runton............. 27 TG14
West Thurrock........... 12 TQ57
West Wellow............. 10 SU21
West Wickham........... 12 TQ36
West Wittering.......... 11 SZ79
West Witton............. 40 SE08
West Woodburn......... 45 NY88
Westbury.................. 30 SJ30
Westbury.................. 15 ST85
Westcliff-on-Sea......... 12 TQ88
Westerdale............... 67 ND15
Westerham............... 12 TQ45
Westgate on Sea......... 13 TR37
Westhill.................. 57 NJ80
Westhoughton........... 34 SD60
Westleton................. 19 TM46
Weston.................... 18 TL23
Weston.................... 30 SJ52
Weston.................... 31 SJ92
Weston-on-the-Green... 16 SP51
Weston-Super-Mare..... 14 ST36

Westonbirt	15	ST88
Westward Ho!	6	SS42
Wetheral	44	NY45
Wetherby	36	SE44
Wethersfield	18	TL73
Weybourne	27	TG14
Weybridge	17	TQ06
Weymouth	9	SY67
Whaley Bridge	31	SK08
Whalley	35	SD73
Whatton	32	SK73
Whauphill	42	NX44
Wheathampstead	17	TL11
Wheatley	16	SP50
Wheddon Cross	7	SS93
Whickham	45	NZ26
Whiddon Down	8	SX69
Whimple	8	SY09
Whippingham	10	SZ59
Whipsnade	17	TL01
Whitburn	47	NS96
Whitburn	45	NZ46
Whitby	41	NZ81
Whitchurch	16	SP82
Whitchurch	23	SO51
Whitchurch	10	SU44
Whitchurch	30	SJ54
White Stone	23	SO54
Whitebridge	60	NH41
Whitebrook	14	SO50
Whitefield	35	SD80
Whitehall	67	HY62
Whitehaven	38	NX91
Whitehills	62	NJ66
Whithorn	42	NX44
Whiting Bay	46	NS02
Whitland	20	SN11
Whitley Bay	45	NZ37
Whitney-on-Wye	23	SO24
Whitstable	13	TR16
Whittington	29	SJ33
Whittle-le-Woods	34	SD52
Whittlesey	26	TL29
Whitton	23	SO26
Whitwell	10	SZ57
Whitworth	35	SD81
Wick	67	ND35
Wickersley	36	SK49
Wickford	18	TQ79
Wickham	10	SU51
Wickham Market	19	TM35
Wickwar	15	ST78
Widdrington	45	NZ29
Widecombe in the Moor	8	SX77
Widemouth Bay	6	SS20
Widmerpool	32	SK62
Widnes	30	SJ58
Wigan	34	SD50
Wigston	25	SP69
Wigton	44	NY24
Wigtown	42	NX45
Wilkieston	48	NT16
Willenhall	24	SO99
Willerby	37	TA03
Willersley	23	SO34
Willingham	26	TL47
Willington	45	NZ13
Williton	7	ST04
Wilmcote	24	SP15
Wilmington	8	SY29
Wilmslow	30	SJ88
Wilsontown	47	NS95
Wilton	15	SU03
Wimbledon	17	TQ27
Wimborne Minster	10	SZ09
Wincanton	15	ST72
Winchelsea	13	TQ91
Winchester	10	SU42
Windermere	39	SD49
Windsor	17	SU97
Wing	16	SP82
Wingham	13	TR25
Winkleigh	6	SS60
Winsford	30	SJ66
Winsford	7	SS93
Winslow	25	SP72
Winston	40	NZ11
Winterborne Whitechurch	9	ST80
Winterbourne Abbas	9	SY69
Winterton-on-Sea	27	TG41
Wirksworth	31	SK25
Wisbech	33	TF40
Wishaw	47	NS75
Wishaw	24	SP19
Witham	18	TL81
Withern	33	TF48
Withernsea	37	TA32
Witherslack	39	SD48
Withleigh	7	SS91
Withypool	7	SS83
Witney	16	SP31
Witton le Wear	45	NZ13
Wiveliscombe	7	ST02
Wix	19	TM12
Woburn	25	SP93
Woburn Sands	25	SP93
Woking	17	TQ05
Wokingham	16	SU86
Wolsingham	45	NZ03
Wolverhampton	24	SO99
Wolviston	40	NZ42
Wombwell	36	SE40
Woodbridge	19	TM24
Woodchurch	13	TQ93
Woodford	17	TQ49
Woodhall Spa	33	TF16
Woodlands	36	SE50
Woodstock	16	SP41
Woody Bay	6	SS64
Woofferton	23	SO56
Wookey Hole	14	ST54
Wool	9	SY88
Woolacombe	6	SS44
Wooler	49	NT92
Woolfardisworthy	6	SS32
Woolmer Green	18	TL21
Woolverton	15	ST75
Woore	30	SJ74
Wootton	37	TA01
Wootton	10	SZ59
Wootton Bassett	15	SU08
Wootton Bridge	10	SZ59
Worcester	23	SO85
Worcester Park	17	TQ26
Worfield	23	SO79
Workington	38	NY02
Worksop	32	SK57
Wormit	53	NO42
Worplesdon	17	SU95
Worsley	35	SD70
Worthing	11	TQ10
Wortley	35	SK39
Wotton-under-Edge	15	ST79
Wragby	33	TF17
Wrangaton	8	SX65
Wrangle	33	TF45
Wrea Green	34	SD33
Wrelton	41	SE78
Wrentham	27	TM48
Wrexham	29	SJ35
Wrightington Bar	34	SD51
Writtle	18	TL60
Wrotham Heath	12	TQ65
Wroxall	10	SZ57
Wroxham	27	TG31
Wroxton	24	SP44
Wychbold	24	SO96
Wykeham	41	SE98
Wymondham	32	SK81
Wymondham	27	TG10

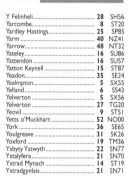

Y Felinheli	28	SH56
Yarcombe	8	ST20
Yardley Hastings	25	SP85
Yarm	40	NZ41
Yarrow	48	NT32
Yateley	16	SU86
Yattendon	16	SU57
Yatton Keynell	15	ST87
Yeadon	35	SE24
Yealmpton	5	SX55
Yelland	6	SS43
Yelverton	5	SX56
Yelverton	27	TG20
Yeovil	9	ST51
Yetts o'Muckhart	52	NO00
York	36	SE65
Youlgreave	31	SK26
Yoxford	19	TM36
Ysbyty Ystwyth	22	SN77
Ystalyfera	21	SN70
Ystrad Mynach	14	ST19
Ystradgynlais	21	SN71

Zeals	15	ST73
Zelah	4	SW85
Zennor	4	SW43